Edith's Cookbook

Treasured Recipes & Women's Lives

Collected by Edith Cleaves Barry (1884 – 1969)

Researched and Edited by:
Leanne Hayden   Amy Tyson   Cynthia Walker

Published by the Brick Store Museum
117 Main Street
Kennebunk, ME 04043
www.brickstoremuseum.org

Copyright ©2023 by Brick Store Museum
All rights reserved
ISBN 979-8-218-23068-5

Disclaimer:

Please be aware that many of these historic recipes are not written according to current health standards, and some will not adhere to modern taste or practice. Awareness of ingredients, allergens, and cooking ability is the responsibility of the reader.

The information and recipes presented in this book are intended only to provide historical information and recipes may need to be adapted for modern preparation and health safety. Many factors can affect how food prepared from a recipe may turn out, including but not limited to ingredients used, appliances used, cooking temperatures (or estimates), and personal cooking ability. These historic recipes are intended for educational use *only* and have not been tested nor evaluated by the Museum nor the FDA. Any outcomes relating to the use of these recipes are not the responsibility of the Brick Store Museum.

*Dedicated to all those
who use history to connect to others and
forge a path forward for everyone.*

CONTENTS

Perspectives & Context:
    Collecting Domestic History   1
    On the Recipe Collector   3
    Where is the flour?   4
    Historical Notes   5
    Interpreting Historic Recipes   6
    The Life of Edith Cleaves Barry   8

The Recipes   10

Recipes by Subject Index   126
Giving Thanks   134

Perspective: Collecting Domestic History
Leanne Hayden, Museum Collections Manager

This recipe book contains recipes from the late 19th century to the early 20th century. It was compiled by the Brick Store Museum founder Edith Barry in the 1930s. Pages from the book, now housed in the Museum's Archives, were scanned individually and reproductions of those pages appear here.

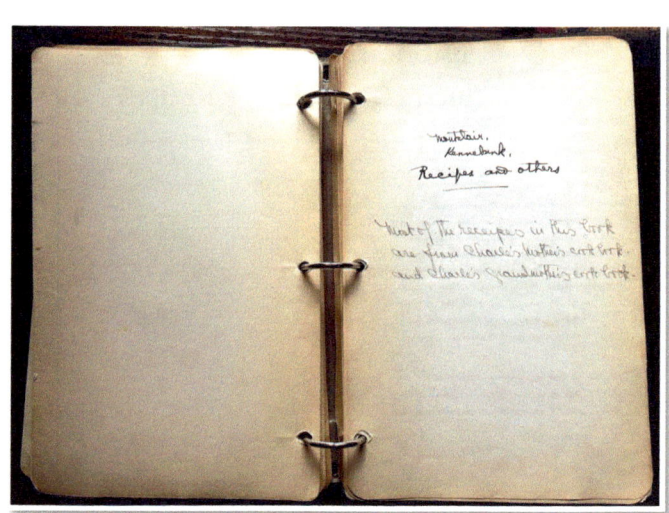

The original recipe book, organized in a black binder, now reproduced for this publication.

Food tells us a lot about family culture. What we eat often defines family traditions and practices that have been passed down over time. Cookbooks will often serve as time machines to explore our cultural heritage.

Before the 21st century, making meals for the family was prescribed as a woman's responsibility. Not only do recipe collections offer an interesting glimpse into historic foodways, they also remain one of the only archival materials (aside from journals) that speak specifically to women's heritage and home work. Many women in the 19th century kept recipe books, and passed them on to female relatives who then added to the collection.

Collections like this one are included in the Museum's current compendium of over 55,000 artifacts relating to Kennebunk's history and its people. As one flips through the pages of this black leatherbound journal, small handwritten notes appear alongside her typewritten recipes to attribute credit to family members.

Edith also collected photos and archival materials from these same family members and friends, and we are often able to match a photo or daguerreotype illustrating their lives. This is a great example of how one artifact can expand and tell dozens of stories. All images found in this book are in the collections of the Brick Store Museum.

Because these types of recipe collections were heavily used, it is rare for a notebook like this to survive. The Brick Store Museum is thrilled to be able to share Edith's collection of family recipes.

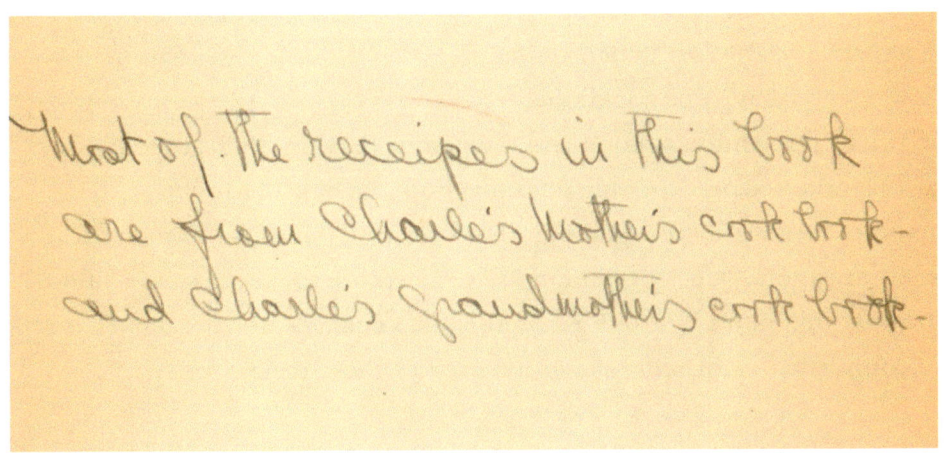

A close-up of Edith's handwritten note at the center of the recipe book, noting: "Most of the recipes in this book are from Charles' Mother's cookbook and Charles' grandmother's cookbook. Charles was Edith's father.

Perspective: On the Recipe Collector
Cynthia Walker, Museum Director

"The meals were very good and well-served," Edith Cleaves Barry often wrote in her travel diaries throughout the early 20th century. While she wrote profusely about art, cultures and experiences, she rarely wrote in more detail about what she ate. Her lifelong slim appearance–inspiring her school nickname "Wispy"–contributes to an initial impression that Edith did not appreciate food for its nourishing or narrative qualities.

Items from Edith's Wheeler School scrapbook, including her photo from 1902 and a cartoon of Edith's slim figure entitled "Wispy doesn't need 'stays'."

Alternative to my first understanding, however, we have this cookbook that shows high attention to food and the people that are often related to a favorite recipe. Not only does this book include her mother's, grandmother's and great-grandmother's recipes, but those women she knew in various stages of her life. As you explore the recipes, you'll find hand-written notes by Edith recommending changes or offering her votes of confidence - indicating she tested each of these recipes herself.

In her meticulous collecting of her family's artifacts, she often carefully transcribed handwritten documents into typewritten tomes (for instance, she transcribed her grandfather's maritime letters and published them for her family). Likewise, she assembled this cookbook to preserve her ancestors' recipes, providing us all a glimpse into these women's experiences, and how tastes evolved through the generations. Perhaps most meaningful is Edith's passion for illustrating women's lives in an era that preceded the modern women's movement.

Perspective: Where is the flour?
Amy Eileen Tyson, Professional Baker & Chef, Kennebunk

When I first read through these recipes, the missing flour made me nervous. How can you make cookies and cakes without that beautiful, soft, incandescent, staff of life ingredient, flour? It simply will not work. The pastry chef in me wants exact measurements, to the gram, and explicit instructions with time and temperature. How much is "butter the size of an English walnut?" Or a "large spoonful of water?"

Upon rereading the recipes, I began to understand that these bakers and cooks relied on their experience and instinct. The flour is there, hidden in plain sight. Add "enough flour to make a thick batter," reads the last line of the blueberry cake recipe. Aha! I therefore must assume that this rule applies to all recipes lacking flour.

Imagine a kitchen 100 years ago. It's quiet. The only sound is a wooden spoon softly thumping through batter in a large ceramic bowl. There is no distraction, just warmth and aroma and sunlight filtering through the window. At least, this is how I imagine life without a digital scale, or a mixer, or plastic. The cook must pay attention to the feel and viscosity of their ingredients. I believe this makes them become more attached to the recipes they know and develop. Note the credit given in this collection: Mrs. Jackson's orange marmalade, Mrs. Smith's blueberry cake, or Sarah Cassin's corn cakes and Mary's muffins. Even the humbly scribbled recipe for a lobster sandwich has a signature at the bottom, "Anna."

This cookbook highlights our community and the women who shared meals and cocktail parties, cribbage dates and funerals. Food nourishes us and brings us together, then and now. The surprise takeaway from this collection, for an adventurous and eager eater such as myself, is the beauty in the simplicity. When entertaining, sometimes a "convenient dessert" of orange segments sprinkled with sugar is all that is required. It is the neighbor you are sharing them with that counts.

Perspective: Historical Notes
Bill Irish, career chef and lifelong historical reenactor, Wells

The significance of a collection such as this is to show the value and historical "journaling" during periods in times of plenty or times of scarcity. It shows us how people adapt and preserve. While looking over these recipes from Edith Barry's family and friends, many thoughts came to my mind:

- Recipes were based on items which were available and grown by season
- Spices were not always available or easily obtained
- Cooks would put their own "spin or slice" on the recipe to make it their own
- Until mass production came to be, wheat was not always available in the northeast
- All ovens "even today" cook differently at the same temperature
- One has to keep in mind that with period cookbooks there was a basic or common knowledge of cooking by all—"dining out" was a luxury for most
- Many references to French early 20th century cuisine
- Dramatic change throughout the course of this collection as to ingredients such as sugar amounts / more wheat flour etc.
- Increase in dessert recipes demonstrating a change in the American diet

It reminds me of a quote by Winona LaDuke, 20th century economist and environmentalist:

> *Food for us comes from our relatives, whether they have wings or fins or roots. That is how we consider food. Food has a culture. It has a history. It has a story. It has relationships.*

Interpreting Historic Recipes

Early 19th century recipes usually consisted of only a few sentences, giving approximate ingredients and explaining basic procedure. They listed very few specific ingredients and mentioned almost nothing about quantities, heat, or timing. The reason for such imprecision was simple: kitchen oven thermometers, cooking timers (much less kitchen clocks) and measuring spoons did not exist.

Instead, recipes pointed to familiar objects to estimate measurements. Examples of these approximations within this recipe book include "butter the size of a hen's egg," "one great spoonful of sugar," or "a wineglass full of water." By the beginning of the 20th century, recipes increasingly began with a list of precise ingredients in numerical quantities: teaspoons, ounces, cups. For most of the family recipes enclosed, Edith Barry updated them to include exact quantities.

The frequent recurrence of cakes and sweets in these types of recipe collections is not random. The availability of ingredients like molasses, cream of tartar, or sugar influenced popular items like gingerbread. In the mid-19th century, items like refined sugar and wheat flour became more affordable and leaveners such as baking soda appeared on the market, fueling an increase in cake recipes and varieties. Additionally, early cake recipes often called for more eggs than we use today because the eggs were smaller. They acted as the primary leavening agent prior to baking soda, saleratus or cream of tartar.

Ovens with temperature control mechanisms only appeared in the mid-1940s. Estimating oven temperature without a thermometer was more of an art than a science! Bread bakers, for example, dusted a little flour on the bottom of the oven after heating it. If the flour turned black without catching fire, the oven was hot enough to bake bread. Because of these technological limitations, recipe writers in the 19th century described only three temperatures: "slow," for thin and delicate foods with low water content, "moderate" for muffins and cookies, and "hot" for crusty breads. Today, many baking recipes are set to 350° F, because when old recipes were converted to modern ones, a "moderate" oven temperature was estimated to be 350° F.

Tips for trying these recipes:

Oven Temperatures:
- Slow oven: 275 - 325° F
- Moderate oven: 350 - 375° F
- Quick oven: 375 - 400° F

Measurements:
- Butter the size of an egg. About 2 ounces, or 1/4 cup
- Wine glass: About ¼ cup
- Gill: about ½ cup or 4 oz.

Ingredients:
- Sago: a type of starch which most likely refers to tapioca pearls
- Saleratus: A coarse-grained baking soda. It's less effective than today's stronger baking soda.
- Soda: Short for baking soda.
- Sour milk/sour cream: Sour milk or cream isn't spoiled but has started to ferment. You can easily make a substitute by adding 1 tablespoon of lemon juice or vinegar to 1 cup milk or cream and letting it sit 5 minutes. Buttermilk can also usually be substituted.
- Sweet milk/sweet cream: The terms "sweet milk" and "sweet cream" are sometimes used to differentiate them from sour milk, sour cream, or buttermilk. It means fresh milk or cream.

The Life of Edith Cleaves Barry (1884 - 1969)

Edith was born in Boston, Massachusetts, on March 10, 1884. Her parents Charles D. Barry and Ida Thompson, both originally from Kennebunk, Maine, welcomed four children: Charles E., Elizabeth, Edith, and Julia. The family moved to Montclair, New Jersey, in the late 1880s to be in commuting distance to New York City where Charles' position at Henry Peabody & Co took him across the globe as an import/export agent. Because of his work, the Barry family traveled the world. This inspired Edith's lifelong love of traveling and her interests in learning. Every summer, the Barrys returned to Kennebunk to spend time with family.

Charles D. Barry (Edith's father) was the son of Charles E. and Sarah Lord Barry. His father disappeared at sea when his ship went missing in 1851 (just after Charles D. was born). Sarah was left to raise her two young sons alone, in a home on Dane Street, before remarrying and moving to 24 Summer Street. Sarah Barry's father, William Lord, made his fortune in the shipbuilding trade: he owned ships that sailed the world and he built the Brick Store in Kennebunk village (now home to the Museum!).

Edith Barry, c. 1934

Ida's father (Edith's maternal grandfather) also built ships along the Kennebunk River: Nathaniel Thompson ran one of the most successful shipyards in the region. As a testament to his commercial prowess, Lincoln's War Department ordered the Thompson Yard to build a ship for the U.S. Navy during the Civil War.

As she grew up, Edith watched her two sisters marry and move away to Vermont (Elizabeth) and California (Julia); her brother lived for several years in South America. In the succeeding years, Edith took special joy in traveling the world with her parents and educating herself as an artist. After living in France and Italy to train with professional artists there, Barry developed her own art and portrait studio business by 1915. During World War I, she joined the Women's Camouflage Reserve Corps of New York City and was appointed to the rank of Lieutenant. Later, Edith bought her own apartment in New York City in a co-op building built by a female designer and intended for artists.

Lieutenant Edith Barry, c. 1918

She spent months away from Maine as her schooling and travels took her to distant places, yet Edith's relationship to Kennebunk continued. She spent summers at 24 Summer Street, and when her Uncle William passed away in 1932, she inherited the Brick Store. Her love for learning and experiences inspired Edith to open the Brick Store Museum in 1936 to celebrate local history and art.

At the age 74, Edith and her best friend Mary Remey Wadleigh embarked on a world tour that they titled "Around the World in 80 Days" in 1958. The pair did just that...circumnavigating the globe in 80 days, traveling from to Brussels, to Africa, to Asia and the Pacific, and then across the U.S.

In her lifetime, Edith funded six buildings to become part of the Brick Store Museum. Today, the Museum is one of only twenty-one museums in the nation to be founded by a single woman with her own money.

The Recipes

Printed in their original order, as collected by Edith Barry

Organization Note:
These recipes are printed in their original order. This means that some recipes are not grouped together categorically and are printed in the order in which Edith collected them over time. Enjoy flipping through the pages of recipes. To find something specific, please refer to the Index at the end of this book.

Research Note:
Great attention was paid to researching the lives of the women who contributed recipes. On the succeeding pages, their biographies are inserted near their respective contributions. Oftentimes in historical research—especially for women's histories—it is difficult to pinpoint a name or person when too little information is given. Notes and information may be inconclusive or incomplete; some recipes with names attached did not offer enough information to find the individual in existing local history.

Bouillabaisse
Provencal fish soup

1 small lobster
fresh haddock, turbot or brill
Gurnet, bream whiting, eel, crab—
altogether two pounds of assorted fish
2 large onions
3 cloves of garlic
2 tomatoes
a sprig of thyme
a sprig of fennel
parsley
1 bayleaf
a strip of orange peel
one half a tumbler of oil
salt and pepper
a good pinch of saffron and sufficient
boiling water to cover the fish. Slices of bread

Method:
Cut the fish into 2-inch lengths, keeping the coarse and more delicate fish on separate plates. Put the onions, the garlic well crushed with the ~~blad~~ blade of a knife, and the chopped tomatoes, in a saucepan, with the oil, herbs and orange peel. Add the coarser varieties of fish, cover with boiling water, and cook for 5 minutes on a very quick fire. Then put in the remaining fish, continue boiling fast for another 5 minutes — ten minutes fast boiling altogether — Remove from the fire, strain the liquid into soup plates on slices of bread, arrange the fish on a hot dish, sprinkle with chopped parsley and serve at the same time. The fish is sometimes put on the bread in the soup plates. The object of this fast boiling is that the oil and the water will blend more thoroughly. In slower cooking, the oil would not mix properly and would rise to the surface. And if the fish is cooked longer, it will break and spoil in appearance and flavor.

New England Clam Chowder

1 quart clams from Duxbury if possible
¼(one-quarter) pound of salt pork
four potatoes
Two onions
1 quart milk
¼ lb of butter
Plenty of Common Crackers
Salt and pepper
a kernel of garlic (if you like garlic)
1 jar of cream (if you want a very rich chowder

Cut up the pork in small pieces and try it out
Strain the fat, and saute the chopped onions
until a golden brown. Heat the clams in their
own juice until their edges turn up(this will
onlt take a couple of minutes) Dice and parboil
the potatoes.
Pour everything to-gether and add the milk and
butter. Split half a dozen common crackers and
float on top with a dab of butter on each. Spear
the garlic with a toothpick in order to take
it out easily before serving.
  It is well to remove the dark part from the
middle of the clam, and the necks, for a company
dish.

From "A New England Sampler"

The Boston Ritz-Carlton Fish Balls.

1½ lbs potatoes
1 lb of salted codfish (soaked overnight)
Three egg yolks
Two tablespoons butter
A dash of Worcestershire sauce
A pinch dry mustard
A bit of pepper

Boil the potatoes, put them through a fine
seive, and place in a warm bowl. Cut the codfish
in biggish cubes, and boil fifteen minutes. Dry
quickly with a napkin, and add the hot potatoes
and don't let it get cold and soggy. Add butter,
Worcestershire, mustard and the egg yolks one by
one. Stir briskly. Shape into balls, roll in
flour and fry in deep fat.

Potassium Soup (Dr Hay's Diet)

½ Peck spinach
I bunch lettuce
I bunch celery
I bunch carrots
few sprigs parsley
small amount very finely chopped onion

Method: Wash the vegetables well, scrape carrots; put in pot just covered with water and simmer over a slow fire for about three hours, remove from fire and put all vegetables through a sieve, add one can or one bottle tomato juice. Serve very hot; the broth in which they were cooked, the pureed vegetables, the tomato juice all to-gether, forming a vegetable soup without meat stock

Rarebit — Charlie Hill

per person
5 ounces old American cheese
I square inch butter
Melt up in double boiler
I heaping teaspoon Guldens mustard
½ teaspoon Worcestershire sauce
little celery salt
add ale or beer to give the desired consistency
Serve on dry toast, sprinkle little paprika on top.

Rarebit

Put one and onehalf tablespoon butter into a chafingdish and melt it. Then add half a pound American cheese, or any soft mild cheese, cut into small pieces, and season it with salt, mustard, cayenne pepper, paprika, and black pepper. As the cheese melts, pour in from a third to one half cupful of beer or ale, pouring gradually and stirring constantly. Finally a well beaten egg is added. Serve on dry toast.

        Marjorie Hillis.

RED FLANNEL HASH

Mix equal parts of chopped, cooked corn beef, cold boiled potatoes and cold boiled beets. A cup or two of each. Add a minced onion, a teaspoon of Worcestershire, and seasoning. Bind with cream or the top of the bottle. Melt plenty of butter in an iron frying pan, and spread the hash smoothly in the pan. Brown slowly, and when the crust form, turn as an omlet. Top with poached eggs.

PORK APPLE PIE * * * DESERT

Fill a deep fire proof dish with tart, peeled apples, cored and sliced. Sprinkle with 3/4 cup of grated maple sugar, half teaspoon cinnamon quarter teaspoon of nutmeg, and a sprinkle of salt. Doth with twenty pieces of fat salt pork no bigger than little peas, cover with a rich pie crust, perforated with a fork. Bake in a moderate oven forty-five minutes.

(Boston) Hotel Statler Rum Chiffon Pie

- 2 egg yolks
- 3 ounces granulated sugar
- 3 teaspoons rum
- 2 teaspoons granulated gelatine
- ½ cup of cold water
- 3 egg whites
- 2 ounces of granulated sugar (additional)

Beat egg yolks, add sugar and rum. Make a soft custard and cool. Soak gelatine and heat until dissolved. Beat egg whites and fold in additional sugar. When they begin to hold shape pour gelatine in very slowly. When light and fluffy, fold in the rum custard and pour in a baked pie shell

careful of the salt — dash of nutmeg
1/2 recipe

Creme Vichysoisse

double boiler

Take the white part of 6 leeks, split and
clean thoroughly, and two medium sized onions.
Chop onions and leeks fine and cook them very
slowly in 1/4 lb of sweet butter. Do not let
them brown.
When onions and leeks are soft add 2 quarts of
chicken consomme and 3/4 lb of white potatoes,
peeled and cut in small pieces. Add salt and pepper
to taste and cook until potatoes are done.
Put through a very fine sieve. Add another 1/4
lb sweet butter, allow it to melt, and if you
want to make the dish extra good put in a cup
of sweet cream. Thoroughly chill in the
refrigerator and serve in bouillon cups with a
sprinkling of finely chopped chives on top.

Evelyn Pinkham

Peas in sauce

Melt 1/4 lb of good sweet butter in a heavy stew
pan or casserole. Shred a head of lettuce into
the butter and add three or four fresh green onions
tops and all chopped fine, a teaspoon of chopped
parsley, a heaping teaspoon of sugar, a salt spoon
of nutmeg, and a tablespoon of cold water.
Let cook for five minutes and add a quart of peas
(shelled) Cook quickly for about 20 minutes until
the peas are nearly done. Then add a cup of light
cream. Season with pepper and salt to taste.
Serve in hot individual dishes and eat with a
spoon.

Mary Sord "Sandholm"

Marion Ruthven Waterston Lord ("Laudholm") (1823 - 1910)

As there are quite a few Mary Lords that may have contributed this recipe, the "Laudholm" note helps to narrow the individual to two Marions who were mother (Marion Ruthven Waterston Lord, 1823 - 1910) and daughter (Marion Ruthven Lord, 1849 - 1910). Marion Waterston, Edith's first cousin twice-removed, married George Clement Lord (her first cousin) in 1846. George became the President of the Boston & Maine Railroad, so the family lived in Massachusetts for many years. In 1881, they purchased the property now known as Laudholm Farm in Wells as a summer retreat near their childhood homes.

Marion Ruthven Waterston Lord (1823 - 1910)

The pair welcomed four children over 10 years, including daughter Marion Ruthven Lord, born in 1849. It is assumed that "Mary" was used as a nickname for at least one of them. As the elder Marion was almost the exact same age (and lived as long) as Sarah Cleaves Lord Barry (Edith's grandmother, pg. 68), it is assumed that the cousins shared much of their lives and this is likely the elder Marion's recipe.

Marion Ruthven Lord (1849 - 1910)

Marion and her daughter passed away within 6 months of each other in 1910. George C. Lord has passed away nearly twenty years prior, in 1893. The family is buried in Newton, Massachusetts.

Mary Lord's Peas in Sauce (pg. 16)

Tested & photographed by Amy E. Tyson, 2023

Julia's Salad Dressing

Mix in wooden spoon
2 saltspoons salt
I   "   dry mustard
I   "   Worcestershire sauce
I   "   Pepper
few drops Tabasco sauce
add teaspoon of vinegar or lemon juice to nearly fill
Salad - spoon . (Taragon vinegar).
Stir, and pour in olive oil until spoon overflows, stir well and continue to use olive oil until you have used three tablespoons.

Have lettuce washed before putting it into ice box, so that it will be very crisp and dry before using.
Rub salad bowl well with garlic.

Julia Barry Bodman

Julia Lord (Barry) Bodman (1887 - 1972)

Julia was Edith Barry's younger sister, also born in Boston before the family moved to Montclair, New Jersey in the 1890s. Julia followed Edith's footsteps to the Mary C. Wheeler Preparatory School in Rhode Island prior to marrying her husband, Dr. Edward W. Bodman, in 1915. The couple moved to Edward's hometown of Chicago for several years in the 1920s before making their permanent home in Pasadena, California, by 1930.

Julia Barry, prior to her marriage to Edward Bodman in 1915.

Despite the miles separating them, Julia and Edith remained the closest of their siblings and often traveled together. Julia held a similar passion for supporting cultural institutions and became an early benefactor of the Huntington Museum & Library in Pasadena, which opened in 1928. After Edith passed away in 1969, Julia fully inherited the family home, the Taylor-Barry House, on Summer Street. She ensured its passage to the Museum in her own will after she passed away in 1972.

Madeleines

¼ cup butter
small ½ cup sugar
I egg beaten
large ½ cup of flour
¼ cup of milk
½ teaspoon baking powder
sifted into flour
almond extract flavoring

Baked in special tins.   Ellen's receipe

Ellen Barthan Magnuson (1893 - 1966)
Portrait by Edith C. Barry, c. 1950

Ellen was Edith's longtime maid and companion from 1935 until Ellen passed away in 1966. Ellen was born in 1893 in Sweden. She emigrated to the United States in 1914 and originally worked in the New York City home of Sarah Woodbury, a cousin of the Barrys, until her employment with Edith starting in the early 1930s. In the 1940 Census, it was noted that Ellen worked 65 hours a week. Later in her life, Ellen married fellow Swedish immigrant Sven Magnuson in the 1950s.

Fairy Gingerbread — Mrs C. D. Barry

1 cup butter
2 cups sugar
1 spoonful ginger
1 cup milk
3/4 teaspoon soda - dissolved in milk
4 cups flour
spread thin on tins with knife

Lemon chiffon Pie

Put yolks of four eggs with 1/2 cup sugar and 1/2 cup lemon juice in double boiler and beat with egg beater until it is a thin custard.
Remove from fire and beat into it one tablespoon of Knox gelatine which has previously been soaked in 1/4 cup of cold water.
Add grated rind of one lemon and when cool and rather thick add beaten whites of the four eggs with 1/2 cup of sugar added while beating, and pour it into the cooled graham cracker crust; which is made by rolling fine 18 graham crackers with 1/3 cup of sugar, then blend in with hands a good half cup of soft butter, then put in a nine inch pyrex pie plate and pat down hard and bake in a moderate oven until the edges are slightly browned. Cool before filling. And before serving cover with one cup of pastry cream whipped and sweetened with 1/3 cup of sugar.

Mrs Fabian.

Ida Morton (Thompson) Barry (1856 - 1935)

Ida Barry, c. 1875

(l-r) Edith, Ida, and Charles Barry, traveling in France c. 1902.

Edith's mother Ida (Mrs. C.D. Barry, as noted on the recipe card on page 23) supported her daughter in every venture, especially her training as an artist. Not only did Ida and her husband, Charles, pay for Edith's education; by the 1920s, Ida traveled with Edith to France, Italy and Germany to complete art lessons. Ida wrote to her four children weekly, oftentimes traveling abroad with her husband when the children were young.

Ida grew up on Summer Street in Kennebunk, across the street from her future husband, Charles Barry. She graduated from Kennebunk High School in its first graduating class and worked to raise her family in Boston and later Montclair, New Jersey, until her death in 1935. Charles had passed away 14 years earlier in 1921. Ida spent the remainder of her life traveling and helping to raise her grandsons (sons of her eldest daughter, Elizabeth).

NEW ENGLAND SPICED RUM

one and one half ounces of rum
heaping teaspoonful of brown sugar
half a teaspoon of allspice
half a teaspoon of cloves

Put sugar and spice in a glass, add rum and stir. Fill the glass with boiling water, add butter ------Sweet dreams Mr Roberts ?

Abbott's Old Tavern Flip

Break three eggs in a quart flip mug [glass], add a teaspoon of sugar for each egg. Stir the eggs and sugar together and add a jigger (1½ ounces) of rum and a jigger of brandy. Beat the eggs briskly while pouring in the liquor. Now fill the mug with beer. Thrust in a red hot poker.

BUNDLING COCKTAIL

1 jigger of rum (1½ ounces)
teaspoon of brown sugar
teaspoon of honey
grain of salt
jigger of lime juice
Shake until very cold

Ward 8 cocktail

1 jigger of Bourbon (1½ ounces)
teaspoon of powdered sugar
juice of half a lemon
dash of curacao
Grenadine to color
a slice of orange
a berry for garnish

CHOCLATE SOUFFLE

3 ounces finely ground choclate
yolks of four eggs
and the whites of five eggs
one half pint of milk.
3 level tablespoons of sugar
I level tablespoon of flour
one and one half level tablespoons of butter

Method: Put the butter into a saucepan, and when melted work in the flour gradually to a smooth paste. Add, very gradually, the boiling milk, flavored with vanilla, stir well. Remove from the fire, and when still warm, but not hot, add the beaten yolks of eggs, mix well, and stir over a slow fire, without boiling, till the mixture just begins to thicken. Add the choclate and stir, remove from the fire and, when quite cold add the whites of eggs beaten to a stiff froth. Butter a souffle dish and pour in the mixture, filling only three quarters full as it will rise. Put in a moderate oven and bake for 20 to 25 minute or till it has risen above the dish. Sprinkle with powdered sugar and serve at once.

ZABAIONE   Italian Sweet

Ingredients:
- The yelk of three large eggs
- One and one-half sugar *dessert spoons*
- 1/4 Pint ~~1 gill~~ of Madeira or Marsala wine

Method: Put the yelks of the eggs and sugar in a basin and beat until the mixture is very light and almost white. Then add the wine and mix thoroughly. Pour into a saucepan and put on a quick fire, beating incessantly, without allowing the mixture to boil or thicken. As soon as it begins to rise, remove from the fire and pour into glasses. When served cold, keep in a cool place until required. Also served hot.

MINESTRONE Soup

Ingredients:

- 3 pints good stock
- One quarter pound salt pork
- one half pound fresh kidney beans
- one half pound of peas
- one or two sticks of celery
- 1 small cabbage
- one half pound of spinach
- 3 or 4 carrots
- one half pound of tomatoes
- one small onion
- a little sage
- one half cupful of rice
- parsley
- 1 or 2 cloves of garlic
- 3 or 4 tablespoons of Parmesan cheese
- Salt and pepper

Method:
Put the stock in a large saucepan, bring to the boil and add the pork, cut in inch lengths, the beans, the peas, the cabbage, and the spinach finely chopped, as well as the carrots, celery, onion, sage, parsley, rice and chopped tomatoes. Stir well and add salt and pepper and simmer until the vegatables are tender and have nearly absorbed the stock. Finally stir in the Parmesan cheese. The soup should be very thick/

BABA AU RHUM

one half pound flour
one level tablespoon of yeast
3 tablespoons of unboiled but warm milk
3 ounces of butter
3 large eggs or four small ones
one and one-half level tablespoons of sugar
a pinch of salt
3 ounces stoned raisins

For the syrup to pour over it: 6 ounces of lump sugar, one gill of water (1/4 pint) 6 tablespoons Rhum.

Method: Sift the flour into a bowl and make a well in the centre. Put the yeast in the middles and with the fingers mix with the warm milk and a little of the flour. Cover the yeast lightly with the flour and let it stand for 5 or 6 minutes. Now add the eggs, which should have been well mixed in a basin, and work with the hands for a few minutes, adding another tablespoon of milk. Knead for about 5 minutes. Cover the basin and let stand in a warm place for 30 minutes. Add the melted butter, the salt and the sugar to the paste and work for another 5 minutes, mixing in the raisins. Grease a mould and fill it only half full, and set to rise in a warm place. When it has risen to the top of the mould it is ready to bake. Put in a moderate oven for about 40 minutes, remove at once from the mould and put on a wire tray.
Make a syrup with the sugar and the water, and as soon as the sugar is dissolved let the mixture boil for 1 or 2 minutes. When nearly cold add the rum, place the baba on a dish and pour the syrup over it. Babas are often made in small fluted cake moulds.

LES CREPES

FRENCH PANCAKES

One half pound of flour
3 ounces of sugar
5 eggs
8 tablespoons of cream
I tablespoon of brandy
a pinch of salt
one and one half ounces of butter
one half pint of milk
4 ounces of finely crushed macaroons

Method: Put the flour, sugar and pinch of salt in a bowl, make a well in the centre and put in the eggs, one at a time, mixing in the flour gradually with a wooden spoon. Then add the milk to which the melted butter has been added gradually, and start beating the mixture. Finally add the cream and the crushed macaroons. Let the mixture stand in the kitchen for at least one hour, and then add the brandy just before making the pancakes. Put a very small piece of butter in a small frying pan and, when hot, put a little of the mixture into it, tipping the pan from side to side so that there is a thin and even layer all over the pan. Cook one side till done, then toss and do the other. Fold, sprinkle with sugar and serve very hot. Hot brandy is sometimes poured over the pancakes and set alight.

The famous crepes Suzettes are smeared with butter worked to a cream with equal parts of sugar, flavored with Curacoa and the juice of tangerines. They are served with hot Curacoa being poured over them and set alight just before serving.
The receipt for Crepes Suzettes omits the brandy, cream and macaroons in the batter.

from Harpers Bazzar

CROWN CAKE

All measurements level

Measure into mixing bowl
2 cups sifted flour
1 1/3 cups sugar
½ cup Crisco
salt
2/3 cup milk
Blend by mixer (medium speed) for 2 minutes
stir in all by itself 4 teaspoons Royal baking pwd
now add
1/3 cup milk
2 eggs unbeaten
1 teaspoon vanilla   or other flavor
Blend by mixer for 2 minutes. Pour into 9" ring
mold 3" deep, rubbed with crisco and lined with
waxed paper along the bottom.
Bake in moderate oven, 375 F   about 45 minutes

When cool decorate with creamy icing flavored
with whatever you are going to trim it with.
A.E. almond flavoring for blanched almond trim.
Orange juice and grated orange peel for candied
orange peel.
Lemon juice and grated lemon peel for candied lemon
peel.
Vanilla for candied cherries and green gum drops

Oatmeal cookies

1/2 cup melted butter
1 cup sugar
1 egg
1/2 tsp baking powder
1/4 teaspoon salt
3 tablespoons flour

mix in bowl, beat butter adding sugar a little at a time egg. beat again till light. add flour mixed with salt and baking pwd. add 1 cup quick oatmeal. 1 tsp vanilla grease baking sheet and flour it drop by spoonfuls. bake in moderate oven 350 - 7-10 min.

Anna

Lobster Sandwich -

1/2 pt. heavy cream whipped cream
3 large tablespoons mayonnaise
4 tablespoons Worcestershire sauce
few drops tabasco sauce
1/4 tsps paprika
cayenne pepper and salt.
Spread buttered bread with lobster
    toasted
which has been sautéed in butter
Cover with sauce and put in
oven. Slice of buttered toast
on top. If wanted -

                    Anna

Anna's Lobster Sandwich (pg. 32)

Tested & photographed by Amy E. Tyson, 2023

Special note: The Museum was unable to locate an individual named Anna without further information.

Rich Cinnamon buns without yeast

3/4 cup Karo syrup
¼ cup butter
¼ cup brown sugar
3 cups sifted flour
4 tsp baking powder
salt
½ cup shortening
I cup milk

place first 3 ingredients in saucepan, bring
to a boil over moderate heat, boil I minute
pour into 9" square cake pan
Mix and sift flour, baking pwd and salt, cut
in shortening, add milk to make soft dough
turn out on floured board and roll into a
rectangle ¼ in thick, spread with raisin - nut
filling, rollup like jelly roll, cut into I in
slices and place cut side up in syrup in pan,
bake in moderate oven, 375 * 45 minutes - let
stand in pan about 2 minutes, invert pan to
remove buns - makes I6 buns

Raisin Nut filling:
    combine ¼ cup Karo syrup, 2 tblsp melted
butter, spread over surface of dough, sprinkle
with ¼ cup brown sugar, 2 tsp cinnamon, ½ cup r
raisins, and ½ cup chopped nuts

Ways to use stale bread:

Cheese Puff

8 slices stale bread, crusts off, cut in triangles
Make pinwheels of 8 halves in ungreased shallow 8" casserole
cut 6 ounces American cheese in $\frac{1}{4}$ " slices, place on top of first layer of bread, cover with remaining 8 halves of bread in pinwheel formation
make custard of 3 eggs
                2 cups milk
                salt pepper paprika
pour over bread and cheese, let stand one hour, bake in moderate over 350# for I hour or until puffed and golden brown

Make French Toast - serve with maple syrup

FROZEN FOODS

Blueberries with fluffy dumplings

Sugar ½ cup
Water ½ cup
I Pkg frozen blueberries
Biscuit mix I cup
Sugar I½ tblsps
nutmeg ½ teasp
milk ½ cup

Mix sugar and water and bring to boil
add unthawed blueberries, cook 3 to 5 minutes
stirring occasionally, Meantime make dumplings
by combining biscuit mix with I½ Tblsp sugar
nutmeg and milk, drop this dough from teaspoon
into simmering blueberries, cover and simmer
over low heat for I5 to 20 minutes. 4 servings

Mexican Chololate souffle

2 ounces unsweetened chocolate
I cup milk
½ cup sugar
cinnamon ½ tsp
salt I/8 tsp
vanilla I tsp
3 eggs

Mix chocolate, sugar, milk, cinnamon and salt
in top of double boiler, place over boiling water
and heat until chocolate is melted (5 to IO minutes)
beat with beater until smooth, add vanilla and unxes
unbeaten eggs, immediately start beating and beat
constantly for I minute over boiling water. Cover
and cook 20 minutes without lifting cover - remove
from heat and serve warm with fluffy sauce - or
whipped cream 4 to 6 servings

Curried green beans
    drop unthawed frozen green beans into I cup
boiling water, cook IO minutes, do not drain,
add ½ tsp curry pwd, I tblsp butter, 2 tblsp cream
mix well season with salt and pepper, simmer a few
minutes longer stirring occasionally, serves 4

Paprika fried chicken and gravy
                  over -

2 lb frozen frying chicken
3/4 cup flour
1 tblsp paprika
2 tsp salt
¼ tsp pepper
3/4 cup fat or salad oil
Milk 1½ cups

thaw chicken and if not cut up for frying, cut up, put into paper bag with paprika, salt, pepper, flour, shake well until chicken well coated with flour (save rest of flour for gravy)
Heat fat or oil in skillet, add chicken and cook over moderate heat until well browned on all sides, about 10 min? reduce heat, cover and cook slowly until chicken is tender (about 20 min) remove chicken to heated platter, add 3 tblsp flour to fat left in skillet (anout 3 tblsps) cook over moderate heat until bubbly, remove from heat, stir in milk, cook until thick and smooth stirring constantly, serve with or over chicken, serves 4 -6

Cheese Dreams

½ lb American cheese
I small onion
½ green pepper (seeded)
Mayonnaise
5 Hamburger buns(split)

Put cheese, onion, green pepper through food chopper, add salt and enough mayonnaise to moiten the mixture so that it holds together, split buns and spread mixture on split side, place under broiler until the cheese is hot and browbed.

* would be good for cocktail party - could use tiny hot biscuits instead of buns.

Rum sauce

2 eggs
4 scant tblespoons sugar
dash of salt
3 tblespoons rum
¼ cup whipped cream

Beat eggs thoroughly slowly add sugar and salt then rum and last fold in whipped cream, serves six.

[handwritten: good sauce recipes in back. foamy sauce, etc.]

Roquefort cheese dressing for lettuce

Crumble ¼ lb domestic roquefort cheese into I pint French dressing

Toffee sauce

3/4 cup light brown sugar
½ cup dark corn syrup
¼ cup water
2 tblesp butter
dash of salt
½ tsp vanilla
I cup light cream

Heat sugar, syrup and water to boiling point, add butter and salt and boil I minute. stire in cream and vanilla, serve warm

Chocolate crispies

I½ pkgs semi-sweet chocolate
3½ cups crisp cereal flakes

[handwritten: drop tsps on waxed paper - chill well - add chopped nuts if liked]

place chocolate in double boiler, melt stir in cereal

Deviled Crab

1½ cups flaked crab meat, sprinkle with juice of ½ lemon, melt 2 tblespoon butter, make smooth paste with 2 tblesp flour, I tsp prepared mustard, add cup cream, cook in double boiler until rich & smooth, stir constantly, put in crab meat with salt & pepper, fill ramekins, scatter over fine crumbs and dots of butter

Creamed hard boiled eggs and little onions served in spinch ring (cut eggs in two lengthwise)

Thin transparent shreds of ginger in lemon jelly, in ice cream, on buttered toast or muffins.*

Corn souffle

I can corn seasoned with salt & pepper & minced onion (chopped green pepper & pimento if liked also) beat 2 eggs add hald cup cream or rich milk, Bake in buttered casserole same as chees souffle

Serve with chicken soup, wheat crackers spread with mayonnaise & chutney. Good idea to add a little curry to chicken soup.

Oddments of left over turkey and ham (or together) set in well seasoned gelatin - like a meat loaf -

Orange sandwiches for tea: ***
    2 tbles orange juice
    grated rind of one orange
    mix with ½ cup sugar, little cinnamon
    spread on hot buttered toast, brown (golden)
                  in oven
    like cinnamon toast - only different -

Rhum raisin ice cream

1/3 cup seedless raisins
¼ cup water
¼ cup chopped walnuts
2 tsp butter
I pint coffee ice cream
I tablespoon dark rum
    Simmer raisins in water uncovered 10 minutes, drain, cool, saute nuts in butter for 3 minutes until crisp and golden
    Let ice cream stand at room temperature until fairly soft, mix in rum raisin sauce, freeze quickly, stirring once only (in 20 minutes) pack in & freeze again - serves 4 -

Easy Desserts with Tapioca

I   Molasses Tapioca cream

1 egg yolk
½ cup milk
3 tablespoons molasses
salt
3 tablespoons minute tapioca (maybe less)
1½ cups milk
1 egg white   2 tablespoons granulated sugar
½ tsp vanilla
light or heavy cream
few drops oil of peppermint if liked

in saucepan mix yolk of egg with ½ cup milk, add
molasses, salt, tapioca, and 1½ cups milk, cook
while stirring (double boiler) until mixture comes
to boil - remove from heat
beat egg white stiff   add granulated sugar - pour
tapioca mixture into this - add vanilla
let stand 15 to 20 minutes to cool, then pour into
serving dish or sherbet glasses. chill in ice box-
can be served with plain cream or whipped cream
with few drops peppermint if liked.

Orange minute tapioca - make same as tapioca cream
but add grated 1 tablespoon grated orange rind and
serve with sections of orange around egde of casserol

Apple tapioca - receipe on package -

Molasses ginger bars

1½ cup sifted all purpose flour
salt
½ tsp cinnamon
1½ tsp ginger
1 tsp baking soda
¼ tsp nutmeg
½ cup shortening
½ cup granulated sugar
1 egg
½ cup molasses
1½ tsp vinegar
½ cup semi sweet chocolate bits
¼ cup hot water

heat oven to 350. Sift together first 6 ingredients
work shortening with spon until soft and creamy
add sugar and blend well - add egg - beat until light
    -over-

molasses ginger bars continued

stir in molasses and vinegar then the sifted dry ingredients and chocolate bits - beat well and stir in the hot water. Turn into a greased and lined 8 by 8 by 2 baking pan - sprinkle with granulated sugar bake at 350 for 35 minutes - cut into 18 bar shaped pieces

Unusual egg dishes   **Stuffed eggs**

Hard boil as many eggs as needed, put in ice
water and press gently to make them apple shaped -
dunk in bath of pink coloring - cut small opening
in ends of eggs and scoop out the yolks.
mash and mix the yolks with half and half caviar
or half and half anchovy paste - refill eggs and
put small parsely leaves to conceal openings in ends
this could be done with deviled eggs also

      hot eggs dishes (foreign)

Huevos Vascongado

parboil green peppers and remove skins
place each skinned pepper in a custard cup well oiled
also oil or butter insdie of peppers, break one egg
into each pepper, dust with garlic salt, pepper,
pinch basil, fine chopped chives cover the eggs with
dry cooked rice, cover eack filled pepper with rich
brown gravy and set cups into pan of boiling water
in oven 400 - cook about 4 or 5 minutes - pepper
cases should start to turn brown.

Oeufs Caroli - cocotte

in buttered small ramikins lay several small thin
slices of cooked smoked tongue -break two eggs onto
the tongue careful not to break yolks - dust with
garlic salt - pepper - chopped parsley - cover with
grated sharp cheese - dot with butter - paprika -
brown in very hot oven under broiler - serve sizzling
hot.   Could be done in casserole for two or three.

Huevos borrachos con Jamon Vina del Mar - Chile -
                                  Hotel O'Higgins
put two cups small cooked lima beans through a sieve
season highly - butter a casserole well - put in a
layer of pureed lima beans - on top freshly broiled
or fried slices of ham (thin) Canadian bacon or
even domestic bacon would serve - break 6 eggs onto
this season with salt & pepper -
in small pan put 2 ounces tart red wine and 3 table
spoons butter, melt out gently - stir well and spread
over eggs - sprinkle with a little mild grated
cheese and put into a 350 oven until eggs are done.

Omlette Cherbourg   St Francis, San Francisco

Make a rich white sauce - about one cup -

Into ½ cup of cut up cooked shrimps add 1½ table spoons white sauce and 2 tablespoons sweet sherry salt and pepper, make a 4 egg omlette in the usual manner and before folding put in the shrimp in sauce - roll up and serve on hot platter covered with the rest of the white sauce dusted with finely chopped, crisped in butter, almonds.

Oeufs en cocotte

put 1½ reaspoons butter into heated ramikins, break into each two fresh eggs sprinkle with finely chopped parsley and chives mixed, add more melted butter and about 1 tablespoon thick cream, dust with paprika and set into a 350 oven until eggs are well set.

Eggs Marigny   Hotel Crillon, Santiago, Chile

frizzle 2 or 3 paper thin slices smoked ham in casserole per person, add six small oysters each which have been simmered in their liquor and sherry top with two eggs each, cover eggs with hollandaise sauce and set into oven at 350 until eggs are set.

Eggs Mephisto   Hotel Copacabana, Rio
garnish for baked or boiled fish - or serve as an appetizer

Highly season hard boiled eggs, pin them together with tooth picks them dip them in egg beaten and then into fine crumbs the latter mixed with small amount sharp cheese grated and paprika and fry in deep fat at 370.

Italian Gnocchi

2 cups water
1 teasp salt
dash of red pepper
½ cup Farina (Cream of wheat)
1 egg beaten
1 teasp dry mustard
½ cup grated cheese
1 tablespoon butter
¼ cup grated American cheese
2 tablespoons melted butter

bring water to the boil with salt and pepper gradually add farina, stirring constantly, cook until very thick) about 15 -20 minutes) stirring well with wooden spoon, Remove from heat and stir in egg, mustard cheese and butter, blend well. spread ½ inch thick in shallow pan and place in refrigerator to chill. when firm cut into rounds with 2 inch cooky cutter, place in shallow baking pan, sprinkle with melted butter and cheese place under broiler until cheese is melted and all is lightly browned, arrange overlapping on hot platter, serves 4 to 6 -

Gnocchi with spinach

2 cups water
1 teasp salt
dash of red pepper
2/3 cups cornmeal
1 egg
1 teasp dry mustard
½ cup grated cheese
1 tablespoon butter
½ cup finely chopped spinach, cooked, drained.
½ cup grated cheese
2 tablespoons melted butter

cook exactly as above, except the addition of the spinach.

Spaghetti Meat Sauce

1/2 lb Hamburger
2 Tablespoons Wesson oil
1/2 cup chopped onion
1 clove garlic   minced fine
1 teaspoon Worcestershire sauce
salt   pepper   1 can Hunt's tomato sauce
1/2 lb Spaghetti   1½ cups water

Heat oil, add meat and brown lightly,
add onions, garlic, cook until tender
Add Hunt's tomato sauce, water and
salt and pepper, simmer 30 - 40 minutes

Boil spaghetti in water as usual until
well cooked - drain in colander - pour
onto hot platter and pour sauce over
Serve with shaker of Parmesean cheese on
table.

Betty Crocker Orange Chiffon Cake

1 and 1/8th cup flour (one cup plus 2 tablespoons)
3/4 cup sugar
1 and 1/2 teaspoon baking powder
little salt
Sift several times into mixing bowl

Make a hole and into it put
1/4 cup cooking oil (Wesson or Mazola)
2 unbeaten egg yolks
juice of one orange plus water enough to make 3/8th cup (1/4 cup plus 2 tablespoons)
grated rind of one orange (about 1 tablespoon)

Beat until smooth, either by hand or in electric mixer.

Into a smaller bowl put the whites of two large eggs should be 1/2 cup whites —
1/4 teaspoon cream of tarter

Beat very stiff - stiffer than for angel food -

Pour mixture of flour and egg yolks gradually over whipped egg whites, gentley folding in with spatular until blended

Pour into an ungreased 9" by 3" tube pan and bake in a 350 oven for 30 or 35 minutes or until the top springs back when lightly touched.
Immediately turn pan upside down on cake rack allow to hang until cold when it will drop out.

Orange icing
   Melt in a sauce pan 1/4 cup butter - remove from fire and stir in 2 tablespoons flour, stir in slowly 1/4 cup orange juice, bring to boil, stirring constantly, boil one minute - remove from heat - stir in one and 1/2 cups sifted confectioners sugar - set pan in bowl of cold water - beat until consistency to spread - stir in one tablespoon grated orange rind. spread on cake.

FISH CHOWDER

4 lbs. haddock or cod
6 cups cold water
1 slice fat salt pork
2 large onions, sliced
6 large potatoes, cubed

1 1/2 tbsp. salt
1/8 tsp. pepper
3 tbsp. butter
2 cups scalded milk
8 common crackers

Cook fish in the 6 cups of water until tender. Then remove bones, skin, head, and tail.

Cut pork in small pieces, fry until brown and crisp, add onions sliced and brown slightly. Add potatoes cut in cubes, and just enough of the fish stock to cover. Boil until potatoes are soft, add fish and the remaining fish stock, with milk, butter, salt, pepper and crackers. Heat to boiling point and serve at once.

Note:- Two additional tbsp. butter may be substituted for pork. If a thick chowder is liked, 1/4 cup fine cracker crumbs may be added to stock.

(Miss J. Scott)

OYSTERS.

To one gallon of solid Oysters, use three quarts of Water, bowl of Flour thickening, pepper and salt, boiled together a few minutes.
Then add your oysters, then a quart of hot milk and butter.

BOSTON BAKED BEANS

First of course, you must have a brown, earthenware bean pot. On Friday get a quart of dry pea beans, and half a pound of salt pork - and be sure you have the molasses on hand.
Soak the beans overnight in cold water; and in the morning pour the water off. Cover with cold water, and bring slowly to a boil. Simmer until you can blow off the skins. Then drain. Put a medium sized whole onion in the bottom of the bean pot. And pour the beans over it. Score the pork and force it down until it just shows at the top of the pot. Add half a cup of molasses, a tablespoon of salt, a teaspoon of mustard, and enough hot water to fill the pot. The pork should stick up a little above the water line so it can brown fragrantly. Cook about 8 hours in a moderate oven. The juice should bubble at the top of the pot all day. When it boils away, add hot water. Serve from the pot with brown bread.

BROWN BREAD

Soak for a few hours a cup of bread crumbs in three and one half cups of milk. Then rub the crumbs through a sieve and save the milk.

Sift together two cups of corn meal, one and one fourth cups of rye flour, one and one half cups graham flour, and two and one fourth teaspoons of salt.

Add the bread crumbs, and a cup and two tablespoons of molasses, into which you have mixed three and one half teaspoons of soda. Then stir in half a cup of raisins, and the milk in which the crumbs were soaked.

Now butter some large baking powder tins. Fill them three quarters full, put on the covers. Put the tins in a pot of boiling water and steam for three hours.
Five tins of brown bread out of this recipe.

FRIGADEL OR VEAL LOAF.

3 lbs. nice Veal, the upper part of the
  leg is the best.
1/4 lb. Salt Pork,   chopped fine.

To this add two Eggs, well beaten,

a tea cup of Powdered Crackers,

1 heaping teaspoonful Black Pepper,

1 Salt and 1 of Sage.

All of this to be stirred up thoroughly
 and baked in a buttered bread pan an
 hour and a quarter.

PICKLED SHEEP OR LAMB'S TONGUES.

Take 25 Tongues and lay them in Salt
  24 hours.
Shake off the Salt and put them in Cold
  Water to boil until soft. Take them
out and skin them, then put them back
into the kettle, just covering them
with spiced Vinegar and about a pint
of the water in which they were boiled,
and just let them boil about five minutes.
Put them in a jar with this vinegar to
cool, and they are ready for use.

POTTED MACKEREL.

Fill a pot with a layer of fish, cut in
square pieces, a layer of Salt, Allspice
and Cloves, until the pot is filled.
   Then fill it with vinegar, cover with
a   crust and bake four hours.

BAKED CORN.

12 ears Green Corn (cut from the cob),
Add 1 pint of Milk and 2 Eggs, a
piece of Butter, Salt and Pepper,
Then bake one hour.

SMOTHERED ONIONS.

Cook the beefsteak as usual.
Cut up six Onions very fine. Put
them in a saucepan with a cup of cold
water, piece of butter size of an egg,
pepper, salt, a little flour. Stew
until the onions are soft. Turn on
the Steak.

RICE

#1

1 cup of rice
1 cup of water

Boil in a sauce pan until a tested kernel is soft

Pour off water and stand pan over a burner until rice has dried.

#2

Put rice in a boiler and cover with water

Boil until a tested kernel is soft

Pour off water
Stand pan over a burner until rice has dried.

(Mrs. G. Croft Williams)
1932

QUINCE AND APPLE JELLY.

Cut small and core an equal weight of tart Apples and Quinces. Put the Quinces in a preserving kettle with water to cover them, and boil till soft. Add the apples, still keeping water to cover them, and boil until the whole is nearly a pulp. Put the whole in a jelly bag and strain.

CURRANT JAM.

6 lbs. Currants,

4 lbs. Sugar,

1 pint Vinegar,

Spice to your taste.

PRESERVED QUINCES.

Pare and cut the Quinces in quarters, with water enough to cover them, boil until they are soft enough to stick a straw through. Lay them in a sieve until cold. Take the water they have been boiled in to moisten the sugar. Boil untill it is a thick syrup.
Let both be cold before put together.

APPLE MARMALADE.

Sour apples chopped fine, one pound of Sugar to one pound of Apples. Grate rind of lemon and white Ginger according to taste. Boil slowly three or four hours.

ORANGE MARMALADE

1 large grape fruit
2 oranges
1 large lemon

Chop fruit fine
Add 3 quarts of water
Let stand over night

Boil 1/2 hour

Next morning add 4 pounds of sugar and boil about 2 hours, testing it until right consistency.

(Mrs. Stuart W. Jackson)
1932

PICKLED BUTTERNUTS. –Aunt Mary.

When a pin will go through them easily they are young enough to pickle. Soak them in salt water a week, then drain it off, rub them with a cloth to get off the roughness.

To a gallon of vinegar put a teacup of salt, a tablespoonfull of powdered cloves and mace, mixed together, half an ounce of allspice and peppercorns. Boil the vinegar and spices and turn it while hot on the nuts. In the course of a week, scald the vinegar and turn back on them while hot. They will be fit to eat in the course of a fortnight.

RIPE CUCUMBER PICKLE. Miss G.

5 lbs. Ripe Cucumbers. Pare. Cut in long strips. Take out the seeds. Lay the slices in a dish, sprinkle salt over and drain. In a muslin bag put 1 tablespoonfull each of Cloves, Cinnamon, Pepper and a tablespoonfuls of Salt, add to Vinegar 1 1/2 lbs. of Sugar. Cover the cucumbers with the vinegar and boil them until transparent.

SLICED PICKLE.

12 green Cucumbers, sliced. Sprinkle them with salt and let them stand three hours.

6 Onions,

1 quart of Vinegar,

1/2 cup Salad Oil,

1/2 cup white Mustard Seed,

1/2 cup black Mustard Seed,

1 tablespoon Celery Seed.

Stir well before using.

Mary Lord Coleman (1844 - 1886)

"Aunt Mary" may refer to one of several women named Mary in Edith's family tree. It is impossible to determine to which Aunt Mary this recipe belongs. It could belong to Mary Hatchett Thompson (Ida's sister), or Mary Mendum Lord; but it is most likely Mary Lord, Charles Barry's aunt and Sarah Lord Barry Perkins' (pg. 95) youngest sister, who lived from 1844 to 1886. Mary was born the youngest of 10 children. She married Walter Coleman and they lived in Brooklyn, New York until her death in 1886. On page 66, you will find a muffin recipe also belonging to "Mary."

[In the image: Mary and her daughter, Louise Coleman]

PICKLED PEACHES.

7 lbs. of Peaches,

3 1/2 of Sugar,

1 quart of Vinegar,

1 oz. Cinnamon, 1 oz. Clove,

Sugar, vinegar and spice boiled together.

TOMATO CATSUP.

1 peck green Tomatoes,

12 large sized Onions,

2 quarts Vinegar,

All kinds Spices,

Black Pepper,

Sugar, 1 pint,

Boil the spices in the Vinegar, then put all together. Boil 1 1/2 hours.

TO PICKLE RED CABBAGE.

Cut the Cabbage across in very thin slices. Lay it on a large dish. Sprinkle a great deal of salt over it, and cover it with a large dish. Let it stand 24 hours. Put it to drain, then put it in a jar. Take Vinegar sufficient to cover it, a little Mace, Cloves and Black Pepper corns, bruised. Boil it together, let it stand until cold, then put it over the cabbage, and tie the jars down air-tight.

PICKLED DAMSONS.

6 lbs. ripe Damsons, to 4 lbs. Sugar

1 1/2 pint Vinegar,

Spice.

Boil well.

BOILED DRESSING.

Yolks of 3 Eggs, beaten,

1 teaspoonful Mustard,

2 teaspoons Salt,

1/4 saltspoon Cayenne Pepper,

2 tablespoons Sugar,

2 tablespoonsfull Melted Butter,

1 cup Cream or Milk,

1/2 cup hot Vinegar,

Whites of 3 Eggs, beaten stiff.

Cook in double boiler until it thickens like soft custard. Stir well. Keep cool place.

SALAD DRESSING.

Rub smooth the yolks of two hard boiled Eggs.

1 teaspoonfull Dry Mustard,

When these are all mixed, add drop by drop, 2 tablespoonfull of Oil, 1 1/2 tablespoons Vinegar.

BROWN BREAD.

3 cups Sweet Milk,

1 cup of Sour,

3 cups Indian Meal,

1 cup Flour,

1 cup Molasses,

1 teaspoon Soda,

Salt.

To be stirred up and steamed three hours.

CORN CAKE.

1 cup Sour Milk,

1 cup Sweet Milk,

1 cup Flour,

2 cups Meal,

1 teaspoon Saleratus,

Molasses, Salt.

RYE CAKES. <u>Very nice</u>.

1/2 cup Molasses,

2 Eggs,

Tablespoonful Butter.

Beat together, and add 1 pint Sour Milk, teaspoonful Saleratus, little Salt.

Thicken with Rye Meal, and bake in small tin.

BROWN BREAD.

1 pint sifted Corn Meal,

1 pint unsifted Rye,

2/3 cup Molasses,

1/2 cup liquid Coffee,

1 teaspoon Salt,

1 heaping teaspoon Soda,

Milk to a rather stiff batter, with sour milk or buttermilk. Steam three hours.

PARKER HOUSE ROLLS.

Take two quarts of flour. Rub in a small piece of lard. Set it away. Scald a pint of Milk, let it cool. At night take half a cup of Yeast and large spoonful of Sugar, and mix it with the Milk. Make a hole in the middle of the Flour, and let it stay without mixing the flour until the next morning.

The next morning, stir in the flour and let it rise till noon. At noon knead and make into biscuit. Bake 25 minutes.

BROWN BREAD.

3 cups of Indian Meal,

2 cups of Rye,

1 pint of Warm Water,

2 spoons of Molasses,

Salt.

1/2 cup Yeast.

Steam three hours.

BUNS.

1 pint Flour,

1/2 pint of Milk,

1/2 pint of Yeast,

1/2 pint Sugar,

1/2 pint Butter,

Nutmeg,

1 Egg, yolk of another.

Use the white, with a little Molasses to put over the tops just before putting in the oven. To be raised overnight.

COOKIES, MOLASSES.

2 cups of Molasses,

1/2 cup Sugar,

Piece of Butter size of an Egg,

Boil ten minutes.

Tablespoonfull of Soda in half cup of Water,

Ginger.

SUSIE'S COOKIES.

2 cups Sugar,

1 cup Butter,

3 Eggs,

1/2 cup Milk,

1/2 teaspoon Soda,

Ginger.

SARAH CASSIN'S CORN CAKE.

2/3 pt. Sweet Milk,

1 Egg, beaten with one large spoonful Sugar,

Large teaspoonful Cream Tartar,

Small one of Soda,

Indian Meal enough to make a thick batter.

PANCAKES.

1 cup of Sugar,

1 cup of Milk,

1 Egg,

2 small teaspoons Cream Tartar,

1 small Soda,

Nutmeg, Salt, Make a thick batter with Flour.

FLANNEL CAKES.

3 cups of Flour,

A large spoonful of Butter,

1 spoonful of Sugar,

1 Egg,

2 teaspoons of Cream Tartar,

1/2 teaspoon Soda,

Milk enough to make a stiff batter to drop. Butter, sugar, salt, cream tartar and soda rubbed together and mix with flour. the white of the egg beaten to a froth, add the yolk and beat all together.

EGG CAKE.

1 pint Water,

1 Egg,

Salt,

1 1/2 Flour.

SALLY LUND.

1 quart of Flour,

1 pint of Milk,

2 Eggs,

2 spoons Sugar,

2 spoons Butter,

2 teaspoons Cream Tartar,

1 Soda,

Salt.

FARMINGTON CORN CAKE.

2 cups Milk,

1 cup Flour,

1 Egg,

1 tablespoonfull Sugar,

1/2 teaspoon Cream Tartar,

1/2 teaspoon Soda, mixed with sweet milk, made thin and baked quick.

IRISH BREAKFAST CAKES.

2 cups sifted Meal,

2 cups Flour,

1 cup Sugar,

2 cups Sour Milk,

1 teaspoon Soda,

Salt.

RYE MUFFINS.

1 cup Sour Milk,

1/2 cup Sugar,

2 Eggs,

1 cup Rye Meal,

1 cup Flour,

1 teaspoon Soda,

Salt.

ONE-EGG TEA CAKE.

1 Egg,

4 tablespoonfuls White Sugar,

1 spoonful Butter,

1 gill Milk,

1 teaspoonful Yeast Powder, and

Flour enough to make it the consistency of Pound Cake.

MARY'S MUFFINS.

2 cups of Milk,

1/2 cup Yeast,

1/2 cup Sugar,

2 Eggs,

Butter size of hen's egg,

Teaspoon Salt,

Flour to make a thick batter.

Keep warm.

WHEAT CAKES.

1 pint of Water,

1 Egg,

1 great spoonfull of Sugar,

1 cup Flour,

2 cups Wheat,

1 teaspoon Soda,

2 Cream Tartar.

BREAKFAST CAKES.

1 cup Rye,

1 cup Indian Meal,

Tablespoonful of Molasses,

Salt.

Scald over night. In the morning dissolve a piece of Soda the size of a pea, and stir in before baking.

JENNY LIND CAKE.

1 cup of Butter,

2 cups of Sugar,

6 Eggs,

1 cup Sweet Milk,

4 cups of Flour,

1 teaspoon Soda,

2 teaspoons Cream Tartar.

Beat the eggs separately, adding the whites the last thing. Flavor with lemon.

CHOCOLATE FROSTING.

1 cup grated Chocolate,

2 cups of brown Sugar,

1 wineglass water,

Crease it while warm. Rub the top with a knife.

LADY'S CAKE.

1/2 cup Butter,

1/2 cup Sugar,

Whites 4 Eggs,

1/2 cup Milk,

1 teaspoon Cream Tartar,

1/2 Soda,

2 cups Flour.

Sarah (Lord) Barry Perkins (1821 - 1904)

Though no recipe in this book is noted as specifically Sarah's, Edith's handwritten note indicated that the majority belonged to either Sarah or Sarah's mother. Since the Jenny Lind Cake (previous page) would have been popular in Sarah's lifetime, it is assumed that this may have been a part of her collection.

Sarah, who was Edith's grandmother, grew up as the eldest child of William Lord and his wife, Sarah Cleaves. She spent her whole life here in Kennebunk, and many of her friends and relatives are named in this book.

Sarah (Lord) Barry Perkins, c. 1850

At age 24 she married Captain Charles Barry, a ship captain from Boston. They lived at their home on Dane Street as Charles continued his sailing career. During their courtship and later marriage, the pair exchanged hundreds of letters while apart. They welcomed two sons, William and Charles (Edith's father). In 1851, Charles Barry was lost at sea after complaining to his wife of troubles with his newest assignment. Left with two young sons, Sarah Barry remarried in 1858. Her second husband, Jott Perkins, was 20 years her senior, and paid for both of her sons to attend prestigious schools in New England. During this time, Sarah trained herself as a painter and was an avid flower-presser. After Jott's death in 1871, Sarah lived in their home at 22 Summer Street until her death in 1904.

CREAM CAKES - Inside.

2 cups of Sugar,

1 cup Flour,

4 Eggs,

1 quart of Milk,

Eggs, sugar and flour to be well beaten together, the milk to be boiled. While boiling, stir in the sugar, eggs and flour. Let it boil till quite thick, when cool flavor to the taste. Let the cakes cool before putting the mixture in. Open at the side.

CREAM CAKES - Outside.

1/2 pound Butter,

3/4 pound Flour,

1 pint of Water.

Boil the water and butter together, then stir in the flour while boiling. Let it cool, after which stir in 10 Eggs, well beaten, the whites beaten together to a froth. 1/2 teaspoon Soda.

Grease your pans well. Drop a large spoonfull, leaving space for them to rise. Bake 15 minutes.

GINGER SNAPS.

2 cups Molasses,

1/2 cup Sugar. Boil 10 minutes, then add a piece of butter as large as a hen's egg, a large spoonful Soda and one of Ginger. Flour to roll.

NEWTON HARD GINGERBREAD.

1 cup Butter,

3 cups Sugar,

1 cup Milk,

1 teaspoon Soda, Seeds,--

COOKIES.

3 cups Molasses,

1 cup Lard,

1/2 cup Cold Water,

Great spoonful Soda,

Ginger, Seed.

HERMITS.

3 Eggs,

1 cup of Butter,

1 1/2 cup Sugar,

1 cup chopped Raisins,

1/2 cup Milk,

1 teaspoon Soda,

1 teaspoon Clove,

1 Cinnamon and Nutmeg.

Roll out like Cookies.

MRS. DUMMER'S COOKIES.

1 cup Butter,

1 1/2 cup Sugar,

1 Egg,

1/2 teaspoonful Soda, dissolved in half cup Milk,

Roll out. Sprinkle sugar over and roll in before cutting.

TERRY'S GINGERBREAD.

1 cup Molasses,

2 Eggs,

2 spoons Butter or Lard,

2 full cups Flour,

1 teaspoonfull Soda, dissolved in two spoonsfull Water,

2 teaspoons Cream Tartar.

Almira (Cleaves) Dummer (1806 - 1886)

Almira and her sister Sarah Cleaves Lord (1801 - 1855), the wife of William Lord (and Edith's great-grandmother, pg. 95), grew up in Saco. The sisters both married local men; Almira married Charles Dummer in 1827 in Biddeford.

They lived in Washington D.C. during her husband's career as a Clerk in the U.S. Treasury Department before moving to Hallowell, Maine, by 1860. Almira lived the remainder of her life there. Charles Dummer Barry (Edith's father) is named for Almira's husband, his grand-uncle. Almira's gelatine pudding recipe can be found on pg. 115.

Molasses Drop Cookies

½ cup sugar
2 tablespoons of butter
1 egg
½ cup molasses
½ "   milk
1 teaspoon ginger
1   "   soda
3 cups pastry flour

Cream butter and sugar together; add beaten egg, molasses, and milk.
Sift ginger, soda, and flour together and add to mixture.
Mix well and drop from a teaspoon on a buttered sheet, two inches apart.
Bake in a moderately hot oven about ten minutes.

Edith C. Barry

Edith's Molasses Drop Cookies (pg. 73)

Tested & photographed by Amy E. Tyson, 2023

Edith Cleaves Barry (1884 - 1969)

See an introduction to Edith Barry's life on page 8.

Photograph, c. 1904

Photograph, c. 1945

Maccaroons

Beat to-gether 2 cups flour, ½ cup butter, 1 cup sugar, 1 egg. Stir the mixture together, flour with almond, make in small cakes, dip in dry sugar, bake brown.

Salad Dressing

Yolks of 2 raw eggs, mixed with one teaspoon raw mustard, oil put in gradually until quite thick, thin it with vinegar until it is as thick as cream, add teaspoon of salt, pepper to taste. 1 cup Lucca oil for this quantity.

Lobster Salad

Chop the meat of the lobster coarse, add a little vinegar, and let it stand a few hours. Chop some celery and lettuce, add this with the salad dressing the last thing.

Chicken Salad

Made the same as above, using chicken meat instead of lobster.

Fruit Cake

3 eggs
1 cup butter
¼ cup of molasses
2 cups brown sugar
1 cup sweet milk
1½ cups chopped raisins
4 cups flour
1 teaspoon soda, cloves, cinnamon, nutmeg

Delicate Cake

1½ cups sugar
½ cup butter
2 cups flour
½ cup milk
whites of 4 eggs
1 teaspoon cream of tartar
¼ teaspoon soda.

HARD GINGERBREAD.

1 1/2 lbs. Flour,

1/2 lb. Butter,

3/4 lb. Sugar,

Carraway Seed, Ginger,
4 Eggs.

DOUGHNUTS.

2 cups of Sugar,

1 cup of Milk,

1 Egg,

1 spoon of Butter,

1/2 teaspoon Soda,

1 teaspoon Cream Tartar,

Salt and Spice.

ELLEN COOKIES.

2 cups Sugar,

2 Eggs,

1/2 cup Milk,

1 cup of Butter,

1 teaspoon Soda,

Nutmeg.

Hot-water gingerbread

2 cups flour
½ tablespoon ground ginger
½ teaspoon salt
1 teaspoon soda
1 cup molasses
½ " hot water
2 tablespoons melted butter or other fat

Mix and sift dry ingredients. Add molasses and water slowly, beating constantly to prevent lumping. Add butter and mix thoroughly. Pour into a well-greased shallow pan and bake in a moderate oven about 25 minutes.
Test gingerbread with a wooden skewer; if done, skewer will come out clean, with no batter sticking to it.
Take from pan and divide with a fork or break in pieces, but do not use a knife while hot.

Edith C. Barry

MOLASSES GINGERBREAD.

1 cup Sugar,

1/2 cup Molasses,

Small piece Butter,

1 cup Sweet Milk,

1 Egg,

1 teaspoon Cream Tartar,

1 teaspoon Saleratus,

1 tablespoon Ginger,

Make thick enough to drop on buttered tin.

DOUGHNUTS--NORRIDGEWOCK.

2 cups Sour Milk,

1 cup Sugar,

1 Egg,

1 teaspoonful Soda.

MISS SMITH'S BLUEBERRY CAKE.

1 pint Sour Milk,

2 quarts Berries,

1 cup Molasses,

1 Egg,

2 teaspoonsfull Soda,

Little Shortening.

ANGEL FOOD CAKE

Measure the following after sifting:
1 1/2 cups granulated sugar, sifted 4 times
1 cup flour and 1 teasp. cream of tartar,
sifted 4 times
Whites of 11 eggs beaten until they will
stay in inverted bowl

Gradually fold into eggs, the sugar, then
the flour
Flavor with 1 teasp. bitter almond extract

Bake in ungreased pan in cool oven, baking
very slowly for about 55 minutes

When done turn pan with cake in upside-down
to cool

(Mrs. Charles R. Bissell)

Use an angel food cake pan

Bake **very slowly** for about one hour

(Mrs. Charles R. Bissell)
1933

CAKE.

1 1/2 cup Sugar,

3 1/2 Flour,

1 Milk,

2 tablespoonsfull Butter,

1 teaspoonfull Soda,

2 Cream Tartar,

1 Egg.

GRAHAM CAKE.

2 cups Sugar,

3 Flour,

1 Milk,

2 Eggs,

1 tablespoonfull Butter,

1 teasoon Soda,

2 Cream Tartar,

Spice.

CUP CAKE.

2 cups Sugar,

3 cups Flour,

1/2 cup Butter,

3 Eggs,

1 cup Milk,

Soda,   Cream Tartar.

COLD WATER CAKE.

2 cups Sugar,

1/2 cup Molasses,

1 cup Water,

1 teaspoon Soda

2 cups Fruit,

3/4 cup Butter,

Spice.

COLD WATER CAKE.

1 quart Flour,

2 cups Sugar,

2 cups Water,

2 Eggs,

2 teaspoons Soda,

4 Cream Tartar,

2 spoons Butter.

COLD WATER SPONGE CAKE-Sarah Hartley's.

3 cups Sugar,

6 Eggs,

3 cups Flour,

2 teaspoons Cream Tartar,

1 small teaspoon Soda,

1 cup Cold Water,

1 teaspoon Essence Lemon,

The eggs should be beaten alone, then add the sugar and beat very thoroughly, then add flour with cream tartar. Last of all add cold water, with the soda dissolved in the water. Beat about five minutes. Bake half an hour.

COLD WATER CAKE.

1 quart Flour,

2 cups Sugar,

2 Eggs,

2 teaspoons Soda,

4 Cream Tartar,

2 spoons Butter.

FROZEN CUSTARD.

Take a quart of milk and dissolve white sugar enough in it to make it very sweet. Scald it well, beat 4 eggs, and while the milk is boiling hot pour it on the eggs, stirring it briskly at the time. Flavor with vanilla or lemon to your taste.

A gallon of milk is abundant for 30 persons, dished in saucers very profusely.

To freeze it, take a water pail, pack in snow 3 or 4 inches deep. Sprinkle on salt, then put in your tin pail and pack closely round the sides with snow and salt alternately. Stir or twirl round your tin pail often, to prevent its freezing in flakes. It can be made the day before it is used, if kept in a cool place.

COCOANUT DESSERT.

Oranges peeled and cut up in fine pieces, with sugar - *sprinkle generously with grated cocoanut - serve very cold.*

DAYTON CAKE.

2 cups of Sugar,

1 cup of Butter,

5 Eggs,

1/2 cup of Milk,

3 1/2 cups of Flour,

1 teaspoon Cream Tartar,

1/2 teaspoon Soda.   Salt.

BANGOR WASHINGTON PIE.

1/4 cup Butter,

1 cup Sugar,

A little scanty half cup of Milk,

1 Egg,

2 cups Flour,

1/2 teaspoon Soda,

1 Cream Tartar.

DOUGHNUTS.

1 heaping cup Sugar,

1 Egg,

1 cup of Milk,

Small piece of Butter,

1 teaspoon Cream Tartar,

1/2 Soda, Salt, Nutmeg.

FRENCH CAKE.

2 Eggs (Take out one of the whites) Beat the yolks and one white separately.

1/4 cup Butter, warmed and beaten to a cream.

1 scant cup of Sugar,

3/4 cup of Milk,

1 1/2 cups Flour,

1 teaspoon Cream Tartar, 1/2 of Soda, both mixed in the flour.

Pinch of Salt,   Flavor with Lemon.

After the butter is beaten to a cream, add, little by little, the eggs, then the sugar, then the milk, then the flour.   Beat all together and put in a buttered tin. Make the frosting of the white of the egg.

FRUIT CAKE.

3 Eggs,

1 cup of Butter,

1/4 cup Molasses,

2 cups Brown Sugar,

1 cup Sweet Milk,

1 1/2 cups chopped Raisins,

4 cups Flour,

1 teaspoon Soda,

Cloves, Cinnamon, Nutmeg.

FRENCH LOAF CAKE--Mrs. Titcomb.

5 cups Powdered Sugar,

3 cups of Butter,

2 cups of Milk,

6 Eggs,

10 cups Flour,

3 Nutmegs,

Small teaspoon Soda,

1 pound Raisins,

Quarter pound Citron.

LEMON CAKE.

4 cups Flour,

3 cups Sugar,

1 Sweet Milk,

5 Eggs,

1 cup Butter,

The peel of one Lemon and the juice of two,

1 teaspoon of Soda,

Beat the yolks and whites separately- the butter and sugar together, then add the eggs, the milk, the flour, and finally the lemon, grate the rind.

Mary Wise Titcomb (1824 - 1887)

Mary was born in Kennebunk in 1824 to her parents William Wise and Jane Perkins. At age 28 she married Joseph Titcomb, who made his career in the maritime trade and building ships in Kennebunk. Their distinct Italianate home, built in 1855, still stands at 35 Summer Street. Mary was a contemporary of Sarah Barry Perkins (pg. 68) and the pair were likely friends, considering they both grew up in town and lived diagonally across the street from each other by the late 1850s. Mary suffered the deaths of two infants before raising two more children to adulthood. She passed away in 1887 and is buried in Hope Cemetery.

ICE CREAM CAKE.

1 cup Sugar,

2 cups Flour,

1/2 cup Milk,

3 Eggs, (whites beaten separately)

1/2 cup Butter,

1 teaspoonfull Cream Tartar,

1/2 Soda,

Flavor with Vanilla.

SPICE CAKE.

1 cup of Sugar,

1/2 cup of Butter,

1 cup of Sour Milk,

1 Egg,

1 teaspoonfull Soda,

1/2 Currants or Raisins,

3 cups Flour,

1/2 teaspoonfull Cloves,

1 teaspoonfu Cinnamon and Nutmeg.

POVERTY CAKE.

1 Egg,

2 cups Sugar,

1/2 cup Butter,

3 Flour,

1 Milk,

2 teaspoons Cream Tartar,

1 Soda,

Essence Lemon.

RICH FRUIT CAKE.

1 3/4 lbs. Sugar,

1 3/4 lbs. Butter,

1 3/4 lbs. Flour,

3 lbs. Raisins (stoned),

2 lbs. Currants,

15 Eggs,

1 lb. Citron,

1/2 pint Brandy,

Spice to taste.

LEMON CAKE.

5 cups of Flour,

4 Eggs,

3 cups Sugar,

1 cup Butter,

1 cup Milk,

1 teaspoon Soda, dissolved in Milk,

2 small teaspoons Cream Tartar, put in the flour,

Beat the whites and yolks separately,

1/2 pound Currants will do.

Season with Lemon or Nutmeg.

MRS. MOODY'S FRUIT CAKE.

2 cups Butter,

4 1/2 cups Flour,

3 cups Sugar,

5 Eggs,

1/2 cup boiled Molasses,

2 lbs. Raisins,

2 lbs. Currants,

1 Citron.

1/4 teaspoon Soda dissolved in a wine-glass of Brandy.

Mace, Cloves, Salt, Cinnamon.

Mary Wise Moody (1840 - 1923)

Mary, who is Mary Wise Titcomb's second cousin (pg. 88), married her husband Horatio Moody in 1862. Horatio was a ship captain, so she often accompanied him on travels and even brought her 6-month-old son aboard. Before the birth of their second son in 1866, they built an elegant Second Empire home on Summer Street with one of the first Mansard roofs in town. In 1876 the family boarded Captain Moody's *The Rembrandt*, setting sail around Cape Horn. In a ferocious storm, Mary was thrown down the cabin stairs and broke her collarbone. Her two little boys Harry and George, 11 and 13 respectively, were washed out to sea and never returned. Mary and Horatio returned to Kennebunk, though Horatio died shortly thereafter. Mary lived until 1923 and is buried in Hope Cemetery. She offered an additional recipe on pg. 100.

COLD WATER SPONGE CAKE.

1 cup Sugar,

1 cup Cold Water,

1 pint Flour,

1 Egg,

1 tablespoon Butter,

1 teaspoon Soda,

2 Cream Tartar,

Spice.

CREAM SPONGE CAKE.

1 coffee cup Sugar,

The same of Flour,

4 Eggs,

Small teaspoonfull Cream Tartar,

1/2 Soda, dissolved in 2 Spoons of Milk.

Salt.

CREAM.

2 spoons Corn Starch,

2 Sugar,

1/2 pint Milk,

Milk to be almost boiling when stir in the corn starch and egg.

Essence Lemon.

BERWICK SPONGE CAKE.

Beat 3 Eggs two minutes, then add

2 cups of Sifted Sugar, beat 5 minutes,

1 cup of Flour with 1 teaspoon of
Cream of Tartar in it, one minute,

Then add 1/2 cup of Cold Water and
1/2 teaspoonful of Soda dissolved in it.

Then add another cup of Flour, beat one minute.

Bake in rather a quick oven.

MRS. WILLIAM LORD'S CAKE.

2 cups Sugar,

4 cups Flour,

1 cup Butter,

3 or 4 Eggs,

1 cup of Milk,

2 teaspoons Cream Tartar,

1 teaspoon Soda,

Season with Lemon.

Sarah Cleaves Lord (1801 - 1855)
Portrait by Thomas Badger, in Museum Collection

Sarah and her younger sister Almira (pg. 72) grew up in Saco, Massachusetts, prior to Maine becoming a state in 1820. Sarah married William Lord of Kennebunk in 1820 at age 19. William became a shipowner and one of the wealthiest merchants in southern Maine. He built the Brick Store—which became the Brick Store Museum—in 1825 as a dry goods store. He invested in Kennebunk-built ships that traded around the world.

Sarah, though not in good health for much of her life, welcomed 10 children in 23 years. All of them lived to adulthood except one. Because of her illnesses, Sarah spent winters away from Kennebunk in Washington D.C. where her sister lived at the time. She left her eldest daughter, Sarah Lord (later Barry/Perkins, pg. 68) in charge of her household. Sarah Cleaves Lord, Edith's great-grandmother, died at age 54 in 1855.

Hot-water Sponge cake (Scott)

3 eggs
1 cup sugar
¼ cup hot water
1 " flour
1 tablespoon lemon juice
grated rind ½ lemon
1½ teaspoon baking powder

Separate yolks and whites of eggs. Beat the yolks till thick and lemon colored, add the sugar and beat well, then add the lemon juice and hot water. Sift the flour with the baking powder and add a little at a time until all is well mixed, then beat the whites very stiff, but not until dry, and fold in.

Bake in a shallow pan or in gem pans about ½ hour.

SPONGE CAKE.- Mrs. Annie Lord's.

5 Eggs,

1 even cup Sugar, to be beat together 20 minutes. Add 1 cup Flour, rounding full.

Salt.

Put in a hot oven immediately.

MRS. MORTON'S COOKIES.

2 cups Sugar,

1 cup Butter,

1/2 cup cold water, with a pinch of Soda,

Ginger.

BLUEBERRY CAKE.

1 pint Berries,

1 cup Sugar,

2 Eggs,

3/4 cup Milk,

Spoonfull Butter,

1 teaspoon Cream Tartar,

1/2 teaspoon Soda,

Salt,

Flour to make stiff batter.

Blueberry Cake (from recipe noting "Flour to make stiff batter")

Tested & photographed by Amy E. Tyson, 2023

Olive Lord Morton (1831 - 1884)

In 1831 Olive Lord was born in Kennebunk to her parents Ivory Lord and Louisa McCulloch (making her Edith's grandmother's sister). She married Dr. Edward Morton in 1851. Edward was a successful physician in town, and the family built a home at 33 Summer Street. Olive welcomed three daughters, though only one, Louisa, lived past the age of two.

Olive passed away at age 53 in 1884. Louisa went on to marry Dr. Frank Ross, also a Kennebunk doctor like her father. Ross was famed for never losing a mother in over 1,000 deliveries. They lived in a home on Main Street, now the Kennebunk Inn. Louisa welcomed four children herself before succumbing to Influenza in 1919.

MRS. MOODY'S SPONGE CAKE.

4 large Eggs or 5 small ones.

1 rounded cup of Sugar,

The same of Flour,

1/4 teaspoon Soda in a great spoon Water,

1/2 teaspoon Cream Tartar,

Beat the whites to a stiff froth, put in the sugar, beat the yolks, put in the flour, soda last.

CONCORD CAKE.

1 cup Sugar,

1 Molasses,

1 Cream,

1 Raisins,

Small piece Butter,

2 Eggs,

Soda, Cloves, Salt.

5 cups Flour.

DELICATE CAKE.

1 1/2 cups Sugar,

1/2 cup Butter,

2 cups Flour,

1/2 cup Milk,

Whites of 4 Eggs,

1 teaspoon Cream Tartar,

1/2 Soda.

MISS PALMER'S SPONGE CAKE.

For a large, thick loaf,

8 Eggs, the two parts beaten separately,

3 cups Sugar, 3 Flour, even full, mixed together,

2/3 teaspoons Saleratus,

Cream Tartar.

SPONGE CAKE.

3 Eggs,

1 cup Sugar,

1 cup Flour,

1 teaspoon Cream Tartar, 1/2 teaspoonful Soda, dissolved in 2 spoons of Cream.

Salt, Nutmeg.

Lucy Palmer (1802 - 1872)

Lucy Palmer lived in Kennebunk as a music teacher and served several local families over the years as a housekeeper. Born in Kennebunk in 1802 to her parents Barnabas Palmer and Mary Place, she traveled northward after 1840 to serve other households in Maine. She never married, but kept significant records via her daily diaries. Her 1838 diary is held in the Museum's archives and details much of her daily life during that year. She struggled with depression but was very strong in her standards, once writing:

> *Have had cause to reflect upon the painful consequences of injudicious and inconsiderate marriages...How much happiness is thrown away - how much misery is endured! Oh Lord! Bless me from such rashness... Suffer me never to connect myself for life with any one where love, congeniality, respect and personal attachment are not the highest considerations.*

Lucy passed away at age 70 and is buried in Dover-Foxcroft, Maine.

TELEGRAPH CAKE.- Mary Hardy.

4 Eggs, well beaten,

2 cups of Sugar,

3 of Flour,

8 tablespoonfuls of Cold Water,

2 teaspoons Cream Tartar,

1 of Soda,

A little Salt.

Have your pans ready and get it into the oven as quick as possible. It needs rather a quick oven.

HARRISON CAKE.

2 1/2 cups Molasses,

5 cups Flour,

1 1/2 cup Butter,

2 Eggs,

2 small teaspoons Soda,

Cup Raisins,

Cup Currants, Ciron,

1 1/2 Nutmeg, Cloves, Cinnamon.

GELATINE FROSTING.

1/3 sheet of Gelatine,

1/4 cup hot Water,

1 cup Sugar, powdered,

Teaspoon Starch,

Season to taste.

Mary Hardy (1859 - 1880)

There existed multiple women in York County, Maine, named "Mary Hardy" in the late 19th century. One such Mary Hardy was born in Biddeford in 1859, to her parents Charles and Harriet. Charles was a manufacturer who moved to the area in 1845 to be the overseer of the Laconia Mill (later part of the large Pepperell Mill campus), which produced textiles. By 1866, he owned his own Hardy Machine Shop, and sent an invention to the Exposition Universelle, the Paris World's Fair in 1867.

Mary died of consumption at age 20 in 1880, and is buried in Biddeford's Greenwood Cemetery.

MRS. WILLIAMS' CURRANT WINE.

3 quarts of juice,

1 quart water,

5 lbs. of Sugar,

Fill the vessel, that the scum may work off let it stand 2 months before bottling.

Research in local history can be inconclusive and often confusing, especially since women's names were often erased by the record books once they married.

On the preceding page, Mrs. Williams' wine is included. In seeking a Mrs. Williams in Kennebunk in the 19th century, at least ten of them came up! The first was Mrs. Abigail (Lord) Williams—William Lord's (Edith's great-grandfather, pg. 95) sister, who married a man named William Williams. Her eight sons each married, and therefore there were eight more "Mrs. Williams." The tenth "Mrs. Williams," named Aphia, was married to *another* man named William Williams, but they were not related to the Lord family although they were neighbors on Summer Street (!). Diarist Andrew Walker even noted how the two men often got mixed up.

To make an educated guess, we looked at how Edith, who edited the cookbook, wrote about relatives versus other people. For close family members or servants, she used first names or full names; for distant family, she noted the relation (i.e. "Aunt Mary"). For those unrelated but held in high esteem, she used the formal "Mrs…" Because the first nine Mrs. Williams were related to her, she likely would not have referred to them as "Mrs. Williams." An additional clue appears on a map Edith had drawn of her grandmother's home on Summer Street (Sarah Barry Perkins, pg. 68). She had noted "Mrs. W. Williams" two doors down. Aphia Williams lived at this address. Hence, it is likely Aphia Williams who shared this recipe. After her husband's tragic death in 1869, Aphia was noted as being one of the wealthiest women in town.

Adding to the mystery, the photo shown above is credited as "Mrs. W. Williams" in the Museum's archives. Because there are at least two women named as such, there is no way to tell which one is pictured here.

EGG NOG

Beat the yolk up and mix with juice of 1 orange

Mix in sugar

Beat white in separate bowl and stir in mixture.

(Miss Alice Bouden)
1932

Alice Bouden (1863 - 1943)

Alice was the Barry family's next door neighbor in Montclair, New Jersey. Alice's father, Thomas Bouden, acted as town tax collector while also employed at the New York Stock Exchange for decades. Like Edith, Alice was born in Massachusetts , and also never married. She lived with her mother in their Montclair residence until her mother's death at age 96 in 1933.

CRANBERRY PIE.

1 cup Cranberries, cut in two.
Mix with 1 cup Sugar, 1/2 cup
Water, 1 large spoonfull Flour,
1 teaspoonfull vanilla.
Bake with two crusts.

CREAM PIE.

1 pint of Milk,

2 Eggs,

1/2 cup Sugar,

2 tablespoonfuls Flour,

A little Salt.

Scald the milk and beat the eggs, flour and sugar together, and stir them in before the milk boils, and then stir it constantly until it is thick enough for a pie. Flavor when cold. Have an under and upper crust.

VINEGAR PIES OR TARTS.

1 1/2 cups Powdered Sugar,

2 Eggs,

2 tablespoonfuls Vinegar.

APPLE PIE.

Take 1 large or 2 small-sized Crackers,

1 cup Cold Water poured over the cracker after being broken in pieces,

1 cup Sugar,

The juice of one lemon.

LEMON TARTS.

Beat the whites of 3 Eggs with a cup of Sugar. Add the juice of one Lemon.

This will make 20 Tarts.

LEMON PIE.

2 Lemons, juice and rind grated,

2 cups Sugar,

1 cup Milk,

2 tablespoons Corn Starch,

Yolk of six Eggs, well beaten,

The above is enough for two pies. Cover the plates with pastry, pour in and bake like custard.
Beat the whites of the Eggs with 8 tablespoonfuls White Sugar. Pour over the pies and set them in the oven a moment to dry and brown.

LEMON PIE.

3 Lemons for 2 pies.
Grate the yellow part. Cut in two and squeeze well. Add 3 cups White Sugar to the Lemons. Beat 4 Eggs and add. Put 1 even tablespoonfull of Corn Starch into a cup of Milk, and add to the mixture the last thing before baking. Bake half an hour. When cold beat the white of 2 Eggs, 2 tablespoonfull Sugar. Spread it over the top and put it into the oven to brown.

MINCE PIES.

3 Crackers,

1 cup Sugar,

1 cup Molasses,

1/2 cup Vinegar,

1 cup Raisins,

1/2 cup Butter,

2 Eggs.
Spice like Mince Pie.

COFFEE GELATINE.

Great spoonful of Coffee to make cupfull.

Cup Sugar,

Cup and half Boiling Water,

Half box gelatine.

SAGO APPLE.

Wash a tablespoonfull Sago. Put it in a teacup of cold water to soak. Pare and slice two sour apples. Boil them soft in a teacup of water, then add the sago and water. Boil till they are perfectly mixed. Add a large tablespoonful of sugar. Boil a minute more. Set it off. Add lemon. Put it in a mould.

CHOCOLATE PUDDING.

12 tablespoonfulls Bread Crumbs,

8 of grated Chocolate,

4 Eggs,

1 quart of Milk,

Cup of Sugar.

Boil it a few minutes, then bake it 15 minutes.
Leave out two or three of the whites, beat up with sugar for frosting.
To be eaten cold.

FROZEN CUSTARD.

Take a quart of milk and dissolve white sugar enough in it to make it very sweet. Scald it well, beat 4 eggs, and while the milk is boiling hot pour it on the eggs, stirring it briskly at the time. Flavor with vanilla or lemon to your taste.

A gallon of milk is abundant for 30 persons, dished in saucers very profusely.

To freeze it, take a water pail, pack in snow 3 or 4 inches deep. Sprinkle on salt, then put in your tin pail and pack closely round the sides snow and salt alternately. Stir or twirl round your tin pail often, to prevent its freezing in flakes. It can be made the day before it is used, if kept in a cool place.

CONVENIENT DESSERT.

Oranges peeled and cut up in fine pieces, with sugar sprinkled over it - dished in saucers like preserves.

Sponge Cake, with a soft custard made of the yolks of the eggs poured over it - the whites beat to a stiff froth put on the top.

A SIMPLE PUDDING.

Boil a quart of Milk. Cut up Bread into small pieces and soak them in the Milk an hour, then add a tablespoon Indian Meal, piece of Butter size of a Walnut, sweeten and add spice.

Prune Whip

10 large prunes
White of 2 eggs
1/4 cup sugar
1 tablespoon lemon juice

Wash prunes, let stand overnight in cold water to cover.
Cook in same water until thick, remove stones, rub through sieve, add sugar and cook until as thick as marmalade.
Beat whites of eggs until stiff. Cut and fold them into the hot prune mixture.
Cook a moment or two and add the lemon juice.
Pile lightly in a serving dish and set away to cool.
Serve with soft custard or cream.

SPANISH CREAM.

1 quart of Milk,

1/3 box Gelatine,

3 Eggs,

1 1/2 cups Powdered Sugar,

Dissolve the gelatine in a pint of cold milk. Boil the other pint and pour over the gelatine and milk. Beat the yolks with one cup of sugar, and flavor them and add them to the gelatine and milk. Beat the whites with the remaining sugar and juice of a lemon, then spread them over the top of the pudding and brown a little.

AUNT ALMIRA'S GELATINE PUDDING.

Pour 3/4 of a pint of Warm Water on 1/4 of a box of Gelatine. When it dissolves add a cup of Sugar, the white of one egg and juice of two lemons. Beat it a few minutes. It will become stiff in a few hours, 3 or 4.

Custard.

One pint of Milk, 2 Eggs and the yolk of the one in the jelly, Sugar and flavor to taste.

STAINED FROTH.

Beat the whites of 7 eggs to a stiff froth.
Add 1/2 cup of Sugar and 1 cup of Currant Jelly.
Beat all well together. Serve in a tall glass dish, with a rich soft custard.
4 Eggs is enough for Mrs. Smith's family.

WINE JELLY.

One box of Gelatine. Put it in a dish, pour on to it one pint of cold water. Let it stand ten or 15 minutes, then pour onto that one pint of boiling water, then add one pint of wine, one pint of sugar. Grate the rind of one large lemon and juice of the same. Strain it through a muslin into moulds.

TAPIOCA CREAM.

After soaking a heaping tablespoonfull of Tapioca in water an hour, put it in a quart of Milk and boil ten minutes. Add the beaten yolks of 4 Eggs, 1/2 cup of Sugar, and boil five minutes longer.
Flavor with Lemon or Vanilla.
Beat the whites of the Eggs with Sugar and put over the top. Brown it or not as you please.

PUFF PUDDING.

9 tablespoonfulls of Flour,

3 Eggs,

1 pint of Milk,

Salt to taste.

Scald the milk and pour it on the Flour hot, then add the Eggs.
Bake 20 minutes.

INDIAN PUDDING.

1 heaping Coffee Cup of Indian Meal,

1 small teacup of Molasses,

Salt.

The one quart of milk to be scalded and the meal stirred in while hot. Bake two hours.

BATTER PUDDING.

1 quart Milk,

2 Eggs,

1/2 pint Flour,

8 Apples.

For plain, 1 quart Milk, 3 Eggs,
   sweetened with Sugar.

SAGO PUDDING.

A mug of Sago soaked in water over night.

Peel and core Apples enough to fill the gottom of your dish. Fill the apples with sugar and pour the sago over.

FOAM SAUCE.

1 tea cup of Sugar,

2/3 cup Butter,

1 tablespoonful Flour,

Beat together until smooth, then place over the fire and stir in repidly 3 gills boiling Water.   Nutmeg.

HARD SAUCE.

2 tablespoonful Butter

10 of Sugar.

Work it until white.   Add spice.

INDIAN PUDDING.

Scald 1 quart of Milk. Save out enough
  to mix 7 spoonsfull of Indian Meal
  and 3 of Flour. Stir in the hot milk,
2/3 cup of Molasses,

Salt, Spices if you like.

Bake two hours.

GELATINE PUDDING.

1 box of Gelatine,

1/2 pint cold Water to dissolve it, then
  1 quart boiling Water,

1/2 pint Sherry Wine,

1 heaping cup White Sugar,

2 fresh Lemons,

Yolks of 2 Eggs, beaten up and mixed with
  about a cupfull of the Gelatine and
  put in a mould to cool for the top.

4 whites beaten to a froth, flavored with
  little vanilla and put around the
  dish when the pudding is served.

Make the day before. Make a soft
  custard to eat with it - 4 or 5 eggs
  to a quart of milk.

BREAD PUDDING.

Soak 1 pint of Bread Crumbs in 1 quart
  of Milk, and then boil a minute.

When cold, add small piece of butter
  and 4 eggs. Bake an hour. Spread
  with jelly.

Beat the whites to a stiff froth and
  spread on the pudding.

PEACH PUDDING

5 eggs beaten separatly (leave out some of the whites)
4 oz stale bread crumbs
½ lb sugar
¼ lb butter
Peaches cut fine

Put in a dish, bake ½ hour in a hot oven.
Put on top meringue make of reserved whites of eggs.

SNOW PUDDING   Hallowell

Pour 3/4 of a pint of warm water on ¼ of a piece of gelatine, when it dissolves add a cup of sugar, the white of 4 eggs, and the juice of I or 2 lemons, beat it well, it will become stiff in 4 or 5 hours. Custard sauce: I pint of milk, 2 eggs, sugar and flour to taste.

APPLE CUSTARD PUDDING

Pare and stew six juicy apples until tender in a little water, when soft mash them smooth, sweeten them, flavor with lemon, and let them cool. Beat 3 eggs light and stir them into I pint rich milk, alternating with the apple Bake about 20 minutes. Serve cold.

Cracker pudding

Split crackers and pour hot water over them, a layer of crackers, then sprinkle raisins with sugar alternatly until the dish is full - two-thirds full - crackers on the top. Let it stand over night, in the morning a custard sauce of 6 eggs to a quart of milk and pour over it. Bake ½ hour.

QUICK PASTRY   *Very Rich pastry*

4 cups flour
I cup butter (chopped fine
I cup lard   (
Mix with ice water. Makes three pies

Common Pastry

3 cups flour, ½ cup butter, ½ cup lard, mixed with ice water.

SUET PUDDING.

3 coffee cups Flour,

1 cup ?olasses,

1 cup Sweet Milk,

Teaspoon Cream Tartar,

1/2 Soda,

1 cup Suet,

Boil or steam 3 hours.

COTTAGE PUDDING.

1 pint of Flour,

1 cup Milk,

1 scant cup of Sugar,

Tablespoonfull Butter,

1 Egg,

Small teaspoon Soda,

Heaping teaspoon Cream Tartar,

Salt,

Nutmeg

APPLE CUSTARD

1 pint of Cream,

1 pint of Apple, (sifted)

6 Eggs.

Baked in little tins.

SNOW PUDDING.

Dissolve 1/2 paper of Gelatine in a pint of boiling water,
Add the juice of two Lemons, and almost a pint of Sugar.
When cold, add the whites of two Eggs, beat to a foam.
Let it stand over night in a mould.
Just before sending to the table, pour over it a pint and half boiled custard

MRS. LUCY SMITH'S PUDDING.

1 pint of Milk,

The yolks of 2 Eggs,

1 large even spoonfull of Corn Starch,

Put the milk on the stove to heat. Take a little out to dissolve the starch in, then beat eggs, milk and sugar together, and pour into the hot milk. Let it thicken to a custard. When cold, beat the whites, drop on the top, and brown.

BAKED BATTER PUDDING.

1 pint of Milk,

3 Eggs,

2 cups of Flour,

2 Apples, cut fine,

Bake one hour. Serve with sauce.

CANDY.

1 lb. Sugar,

Butter size of English walnut,

2 spoonfulls Vinegar,

1/2 cup Water.

CHOCOLATE CARAMELS.

3 heaping tablespoonfulls Chocolate, grated fine.

1 tablespoonfull of Molasses,

1 cup of Sugar,

2/3 cup of Milk,

Small piece of Butter,

Flavor with vanilla if you like.
Boil half an hour.

KISSES.

Beat the whites of the eggs to a stiff froth. 8 teaspoonfuls of Sugar to 1 Egg. Flavor with Rose. Drop a spoonful on to a pan, and bake them a light brown.

CANDY.

1 cup Vinegar,

2 cups of Sugar,

Flavor with vanilla and boil till thick.

CANDY.

6 tablespoonfulls grated Chocolate,

1 cup of Milk,

Butter size of an Egg,

2 cups Sugar,

2 tablespoonfull Molasses.

Fudge, icing, or sauce

2 squares of Baker's unsweetened chocolate
¼ lb. butter
1 cup milk (or cream, with less butter)
2 cups granulated sugar (white)
1 pinch salt

Melt chocolate. (Do not let it burn, or boil, or get too hot.)
Add butter till melted (not too hot.)
Slowly add milk, stirring constantly.
Bring to a boil and add sugar and salt.
Cook to the soft-ball degree.
Take off stove.
Beat it.
Add 1 tsp. vanilla when beaten and cooked a bit.
Turn into a buttered square pan.
Use as fudge, or as fudge cake icing (cooked longer and beaten less) or as fudge sauce (cooked less.)

Edith C. Barey

Recipes by Subject Index

Recipes by Subject Index

Appetizers
Cheese Dreams	38
Deviled Crab	39
Fish Balls	12

Breads and Staples
Breads:
Brown Bread	49, 60, 61
Buns	62
Cinnamon Buns	34
Doughnuts	77, 79, 85
Parker House Rolls	61

Staples:
Frozen Foods	36
Ways to Use Stale Bread	35
Cheese Puff	35
French Toast	35

Breakfast and Brunch
Cheese Puff	35
Cinnamon Buns	34
Doughnuts	77, 79, 85

Egg Dishes:
Eggs Marigny	43
Eggs Mephisto	43
Huevos Borrachos con Jamon	42
Huevos Vascongado	42
Oeufs Caroli - Cocotte	42
Oeufs en Cocotte	43
Omlette Cherbourg	43
Stuffed Eggs	42

French Toast	35

Recipes by Subject Index (Cont.)

Breakfast and Brunch (Cont.)

Morning Cakes:
    Corn Cake   60, 63, 64
    Egg Cake   64, 65
    Flannel Cakes   63
    Irish Breakfast Cakes   65
    Muffins   65, 66
    Pancakes   63
    Rye Cakes   60, 66
    Sally Lund   64
    Wheat Cakes   66
Orange Sandwiches for Tea   39
Red Flannel Hash   15

Cakes

Angel Food Cake   80
Blueberry Cake   79, 97-98
Cake   81
Cold Water Cake   82, 83, 84, 93
Concord Cake   100
Cream Cake   69
Crown Cake   30
Dayton Cake   85
Delicate Cake   76, 100
Frosting::
    Chocolate Frosting   67
    Fudge, Icing or Sauce   124
    Gelatine Frosting   103
French Cake   86
French Loaf Cake   87
Fruit Cake   76, 86, 90, 91
Gingerbread   23, 70, 71, 77, 78, 79

Recipes by Subject Index (Cont.)

Cakes (Cont.)

Graham Cake	81
Harrison Cake	103
Hot Water Cake	96
Ice Cream Cake	89
Jenny Lind Cake	67
Lady's Cake	67
Lemon Cake	87, 91
Mrs. William Lord's Cake	94
Orange Chiffon Cake	46
Poverty Cake	90
Spice Cake	89
Sponge Cake	83, 93, 94, 96, 97, 100, 101
Telegraph Cake	103

Candy

Candies	122, 123
Chocolate Caramels	123
Fudge, Icing or Sauce	124
Kisses	123

Cocktails

Abbott's Old Tavern Flip	25
Bundling Cocktail	25
Currant Wine	105
Egg Nog	107
New England Spiced Rum	25
Ward 8 Cocktail	25
Zabaione	27

Recipes by Subject Index (Cont.)

Condiments & Pickles

Jams and Jellies:
    Quince and Apple Jelly   53
    Currant Jam   53
    Preserved Quinces   53
    Apple Marmalade   53
    Orange Marmalade   54
    Wine Jelly   116

Pickling::
    Pickled Butternuts   55
    Cucumber Pickles   55
    Pickled Damsons   58
    Pickled Peaches   57
    To Pickle Red Cabbage   58

Salad Dressings   19, 38, 59, 76
Tomato Catsup   58

Cookies

Chocolate Crispies   38
Ellen Cookies   77
Ginger Snaps   62, 69
Hermits   71
Madeleines   21
Maccaroons   76
Molasses Cookies   62, 70, 73-74
Mrs. Dummer's Cookies   71
Mrs. Morton's Cookies   97
Oatmeal Cookies   31

Recipes by Subject Index (Cont.)

Desserts

Baba Au Rhum	28
Blueberries with Fluffy Dumplings	36
Chocolate Souffle	26, 36
Cocoanut Dessert	84
Convenient Dessert	113
Les Crepes	29
Molasses Ginger Bars	40-41
Pastry	119
Pies:	
Apple Pie	110
Bangor Washington Pie	85
Cranberry Pie	109
Cream Pie	110
Lemon Tarts and Pie	23, 110, 111
Mince Pies	111
Pork Apple Pie	15
Rum Chiffon Pie	15
Vinegar Pies or Tarts	110
Pudding and Custards:	
Apple Custard Pudding	119, 120
Batter Pudding	117, 121
Bread Pudding	118
Chocolate Pudding	112
Cottage Pudding	120
Cracker Pudding	119
Custard	84, 113, 115
Gelatine Pudding	112, 115, 118
Indian Pudding	116, 118
Mrs. Lucy Smith's Pudding	121
Peach Pudding	119
Prune Whip	114
Puff Pudding	116

Recipes by Subject Index (Cont.)

Desserts (Cont.)

Pudding and Custards (Cont.):

Sago Pudding	112, 117
Simple Pudding	113
Snow Pudding	119, 121
Suet Pudding	120
Tapioca	40

Rhum Raisin Ice Cream — 39

Sauces and Creams:

Foam Sauce	117
Fudge, Icing or Sauce	124
Hard Sauce	117
Rum Sauce	38
Molasses Tapioca Cream	40
Spanish Cream	115
Stained Froth	115
Tapioca Cream	116
Toffee Sauce	38

Zabaione — 27

Main Dishes

Meat/Seafood Dishes:

Chicken Salad	76
Frigadel or Veal Loaf	50
Lobster Salad	76
Lobster Sandwich	32-33
Paprika Fried Chicken and Gravy	36-37
Pickled Sheep or Lamb's Tongues	50
Potted Mackerel	50
Rarebit	14

Recipes by Subject Index (Cont.)

Main Dishes (Cont.)

Pastas:

Gnocchi With Spinach	44
Italian Gnocchi	44
Spaghetti With Meat Sauce	45

Soups

Bouillabaisse – Provencal Fish Soup	11
Creme Vichysoisse	16
Fish Chowder	47
Minestone	27
New England Clam Chowder	12
Oysters	48
Potassium Soup	13

Vegetable and Side Dishes

Baked Corn	51
Boston Baked Beans	49
Corn Souffle	39
Curried Green Beans	36
Peas in Sauce	16, 18
Rice	52
Smothered Onions	51

Giving Thanks

This recipe book was built over time by the family, friends and community surrounding Edith Barry. Like the original recipe book, this publication would not be possible without the significant help and teamwork of so many.

Our thanks to every Museum volunteer who gave their time, thought and expertise to developing and editing this work, including: Mimi Malkasian, for her superior grammar editing skills and gentle advice; Nancy Dorn, for her enthusiastic review of the tome; Donna Griglock for her early cheerleading of this project; Laura Dauphinais for her incredible organization skills indexing the recipes; Elsa van Bergen for her incredibly detailed and professional copy editing; and Cindy Sayers and Lucille Gentsch for crafting excitement around its release.

Thank you to Edith Barry, who had the foresight to save memories such as these and find ways to share them. Thank you further to all of the women (and some men!) who unknowingly contributed to this book simply by cooking for their own families.

Thank you, especially, to all of the Brick Store Museum Members and supporters who constantly champion the Museum and its programs, ensuring that local history has a bright future indeed.

Happy cooking! Happy sharing!

Leanne, Amy and Cynthia